Bright Dawn Dharma Glimpses:

A Collection of Teachings from Everyday Life

Dharma House Publishing
Affiliate of the Bright Dawn Center

Compiled by Bright Dawn Trailblazer Group

Edited by Adrienne Kubose & Tamu Hoyo Ngina

Bright Dawn Dharma Glimpses:
A Collection of Teachings from Everyday Life

Dharma House Publishing
Affiliate of the Bright Dawn Center
Coarsegold, California 93614
www.BrightDawn.org

ISBN 978-0-9642992-5-2

Compiled by Bright Dawn Trailblazer Group

Edited by Adrienne Kubose & Tamu Hoyo Ngina

Cover Credit: Bright Dawn logo Dharma Wheel Sculpture
created by artist Mark Jackson
www.MJackson-Sculpture.com

THIS BOOK IS DEDICATED TO:
Don Akeru Kubose (1936-2015)

My brother Don supported all of our Bright Dawn Center activities. When asked to give a Dharma Glimpse, he would accept with great enthusiasm.

One of his last Dharma Glimpses was inspired by his viewing of a classic 1950's movie, "The Incredible Shrinking Man." In this science-fiction movie, a man is exposed to radioactive events that rearrange his molecular structure, causing his cells to keep shrinking.

The bulk of the movie depicts the many difficulties caused by the man's shrinking size. Near the end of the movie, he is trapped in his basement where he has to kill a spider with a straight pin. He is so small that his family cannot hear his screams for help.

In the final scene, the man has become so small he can leave the basement by going through the tiny squares of a window screen. The man accepts his fate and knows he will keep shrinking to atomic size; but no matter how small he becomes, he knows he will still matter in the universe because in the realm of Absolute Reality, "there is no zero." This thought comforts the man and he no longer fears the future.

My brother told me he thought this ending of the movie was Buddhistic. I agree and I thank my brother for going forward into the world of Oneness and showing us how to "Keep Going."

Rev. Koyo S. Kubose
Coarsegold, California
Autumn, 2016

Bright Dawn Dharma Glimpses:

CONTENTS

Bright Dawn Dharma Glimpses:

INTRODUCTION

Ten years ago our Bright Dawn Center started a two-year non-residential, internet-based Lay Ministry Study Program. Typically, a group of 4-6 students would write reports on assigned readings and then discuss their reports in weekly small-group teleconferences. Each weekly session began with one of the students giving a Dharma Glimpse, which is a personal account of some kind of life teaching.

Currently, there are over forty Lay Ministers (LMs) who have completed the Program. They are using their Study Program experiences in diverse ways in their particular locales. Our LMs live in cities scattered across the country, including in Hawaii, Canada, and Brazil. In addition to helping teach our Program curriculum courses to new students, the LMs continue to give Dharma Glimpses as part of our Live Dharma Sunday broadcasts which are aired every Sunday morning.

Our LMs are organized into a support group called the Bright Dawn Trailblazers which "meets" via a monthly group teleconference. One of their many projects is a compilation of their past Dharma Glimpses into book form, and here it is! This collection of Dharma Glimpses contain insightful "nuggets" that illustrate how teachings can be creatively discovered in everyday life experiences. One purpose of our LM Study Program is to encourage the natural or spontaneous occurrence of personal Dharma Glimpses in the midst of daily activities. After all, isn't the goal of Buddhist practice to develop the perspective that living life and living the Dharma are identical?

Through LM Dharma Glimpses, I have been privileged to see the transformation from just knowing about the Buddhist teachings to actually living the Dharma teachings in the richness of individual experiences. What a gratifying joy this is to me! I am so impressed to witness the diverse ways the teachings come alive! May the sharing of the Dharma Glimpses in this collection similarly inspire readers to become aware of how precious it is to become One with the Dharma. May It Be So.

Rev. Koyo S. Kubose
Coarsegold, California
Autumn, 2016

BUDDHA ABOVE DUMPSTERS
A.Naiyo

While taking a walk near Highway 101in Redwood City, CA, I came across a large statue of a seated Buddha facing the highway sitting atop an enclosure for 2 dumpsters. There was an incense burner and fresh fruits at its base. How curious! What could it mean?

I posted a picture of it on Facebook and also sent out an email with the picture attached to share this unusual sight and see what others thought of it. Here are some of the responses:

William Seiyo Shehan
trash below
blue sky above-
Buddha smiles

Tamu Hoyo Ngina
Even among the trashiest there is Buddha nature

Clarence Genyo
You can grow out of any circumstances.

Mark Kaiyo Fives
Any space can be sacred space. Let your mind be free of labels and find your true nature.

Linda Shoyo
Someone's trash can be someone else's treasure. It's all the way we look at it. Who knows what we might find if we stay open.

Dave Teiyo Pangburn
Everything begins as something new but eventually becomes waste... nothing remains the same, there is constant change. The Buddha is constant. Even humans experience change, but Buddha nature is constant. The Buddha in this photo has transcended change....

Renee Seiyo
What trash? I only see the Buddha...

Andy Goyo Bondy
Some of us stand on the shoulders of giants- some need only to sit on garbage....

Roger Seiyo
Just as the Dharma is everywhere, so are the dharmas everywhere. Just as the lotus grows out of the black muck of decay, so does the Dharma arise from the realization of the sources of dissatisfaction.

Ginny
Yo!! Even the Buddha gotta "take a dump" sometime!
(Sorry...I just was re-reading about Toilet Gassho in the "Bathroom" chapter of Koyo Kubose Sensei's Bright Dawn, pp. 31-37.)

Sayo Shenpän
For me, it's says rise above day to day trash! Or transcend the mundane mind and rise above it! Beauty can be found even in the oddest of places.

What a wonderful wealth of responses! After seeing all these responses and especially the wealth of different Dharma Glimpses in this book, I realize why Buddha said there are 84,000 paths to Enlightenment and for each of us to follow our own path.

Bright Dawn Dharma Glimpses:

LAY MINISTER CLASS
#1

MAKING BREAD
Andy Jiyo Agacki

Turns out, I like to make bread. I *really* like to make bread. Lot's of *reasons* for it, now that I come to *think* of it, but it was all rather accidental.

We needed some bread. We had a bunch of flour and some old yeast sitting around. I'm an adventurous soul. Ah! So, how hard can it be? I used to help my Dziadzia (my Polish grandfather) make bread, but it was mostly sitting with him eating the end result. He just seemed to whip things together and *Voila!* . . . bread. It was all so *easy*!

So off to the laptop to Google recipes. Found a basic beginner's recipe. Just the thing.

That first loaf turned out nice and tasty. Even after many months of experimentation, I *still* use that recipe as my 'go-to' plan . . . though I use it a bit more 'playfully' nowadays.

Lately though, I've come to cogitate over the process and what it all means to me.

When I make bread, I'm pretty 'loose' with the instructions and ingredients. For instance, I don't make sure the temperature of the water I'm proofing the yeast in is between 170 and 180 deg. F. I'm not orthodox; if the water out of the tap is comfortable to me, not too hot or cold, it's fine. Yeast is a living thing. I can relate; most things in my life are inexact, uncertain. I just try to make it as comfortable as possible for everyone.

And I'm dealing with living, breathing *life*; that yeast, and killing it. The extreme heat of the baking process does that. But we LIVE that way too, don't we? Killing animals and plants to survive, at the very least *harming and hurting* life in the process. That sugar was a live plant once, and the wheat. I've become more careful and mindful of that as I bake.

And I have become more aware that my life has to cooperate with everything around me too, for my life, ALL life, to arise and develop.

That's why that basic beginner's recipe is still with me. With all the decades of life behind me, all the loaves of bread I've made, I'm still a beginner at it all, still learning the recipes, still kneading, prodding and poking.

If I can give you one little pointer from baking and my life, it is this:

Avoid the quick rising yeast; your end result will lack for it,
and it'll probably just fall apart in the end. Be careful, take
your time, and be thankful.

Thank you kindly for listening, but I have some loaves rising and I need to check on them. Peace.

THE TERMINATOR
Ricardo Ryuyo Sasaki

Last year, the Dalai Lama came to Brazil for the third time. It was an occasion of joy and sharing. During three days he talked to the public sharing his wisdom and humor. Those present at the events didn´t fail to notice a smiley, nice old man, always dressed with a green t-shirt and carrying a camera able to make jealous any professional photographer present at the events. Also present was Mr. Chang Sheng Kai, a businessman, owner of a cold drinks factory, and benefactor of many Buddhist institutions. He was the main financial supporter of the huge Zulai Temple of Fo Kuan Shan organization.

With his camera, Mr. Chang sat beside me during the talk by the Dalai Lama at Zulai, and not in a special seat prepared for him, considering that he provided a significant amount of money for the Dalai Lama´s trip. While I was seated in a chair, he was happy to sit on the stairs of the temple. With an almost childish joy he took endless non-stop pictures of the Tibetan leader, capturing every movement, every change of expression. I even playfully commented to a friend later on that someone should inform Mr. Chang that people had already invented the video camera, as he took so many pictures that it would be easier just to make a film.

It was a shock, then, when a few days later, we came to know Mr. Chang had died. Immediately, an event in the time of the Buddha came to my mind that I recently had read. There was in the city of Savatthi, a very devout lady who used to do everything for the monastery. She used to carry food for the monks, sweep the floor, fill the water pots, and provided many services for the well-being of the monks and practitioners. That morning, she came to the temple, fed the monks and gave flowers to the Buddha. By the afternoon the monks came to know she was dead, leaving behind four children and a lifetime of virtue and devotion. Shocked, the monks came to the Buddha, and He said, "The Terminator overpowers a man even while he is gathering flowers and whose mind is distracted even before he is satiated in his pleasures."

The Terminator, here, is another name for Death and the meaning of the verse is to show the fragility of life. We live life picking flowers, desiring this and that, but never contented. Then, without any warning, death comes and takes us. What an excellent teaching on impermanence! May we live life the best we can and keep the right direction! Thank you!

SHINRAN AND STEVE JOBS
Ricardo Sasaki

A common teaching in Korean Zen tells about "right situation, right relationship, right function". When we don't understand these, we have some problems.

Many who approach Buddhism have a preconceived idea about it, and even after years and years of study and practice keep some behaviours they think are "Buddhist".

So, when there is a situation of joy and happiness, the person starts talking about suffering and impermanence. These are the 'serious' and pessimistic Buddhists. Others have placed in their minds that Buddhism is not a pessimistic philosophy, but on the contrary, it is the summit of optimism and then start to see every situation, even the not so worthwhile as amazing opportunities and out-of-earth lessons of life. These are the exaggerated optimists and overly (almost manic) joyful ones.

At the time of the Buddha there was a monk who combined both characteristics and was unable to say the right things at the right moments. In joyful occasions he spoke sad things. In sad occasions, he spoke joyful and funny things. In the Dhammapada 152, the Buddha referred to him as:

> *The foolish man*
> *grows like an ox*
> *his muscles grow*
> *but not his wisdom.*

So then, what is it to have a proper grasp of reality?

How to have a contemplative eye, that enables us see the impermanence of all conditioned things at the same time as allowing a new attitude regards good and bad things in life?

Those who practice according to the Pure Land School, know well how Honen was exiled, along with many of his disciples. Shinran was one of them. Shinran, in spite of the hard situation of isolation, privations and so on, did not fall into despair. In one of the classic biographies of Shinran (Denne), he tells how he saw his situation:

If the Great Master Hônen, had not been exiled, I would not have been sent to my place of exile. If I had not been exiled, how would I have been able to teach the people of this remote area (the Way of the Nembutsu)?

In another example completely different, but showing as well the capacity of seeing difficult situations from the angle of opportunity, we have a recent statement made by Steve Jobs, the founder of Apple, Pixar and creator of MacIntosh. When talking about his first years he used a metaphor of "connecting dots". He said:

Again, you can't connect the dots looking forward; you can only connect them looking backwards. So you have to trust that the dots will somehow connect in your future. You have to trust in something — your gut, destiny, life, karma, whatever. This approach has never let me down, and it has made all the difference in my life.

Though separated in space and time, Shinran and Jobs had something in common: they both loved what they were doing and made an effort to see the right behavior for the right situation.

STUMBLING ON THE PATH
John Miyo Wylder

One of the things I love about Shinran Shonin is that he accepts the fact that I'm a screw-up. When I hang out with Buddhists of other traditions, as I often do, our conversations tend to run toward the amazing insights we've had, or the astounding feelings of peace and contentment we've had while meditating, or just how long we can sit in meditation before our thoughts wander. And all this is useful, if a bit passive-aggressive and ego-driven; but Buddhism takes place 24-hours a day, not just on the meditation cushion. And it's the rest of the day that no one seems to talk about, and it's where I seem to have the most trouble.

For instance, have you really tried to get through a real day in the lay world walking just *one* part of the Noble Eight Fold Path? I hope you have better luck at it than I do because I can't make it through eight hours at work, or even the morning. Sometimes I can't make it through the first five minutes face-to-face with my supervisor without stumbling over Right Speech.

At the moment, I'm working at an academic library at a small community college, and not only has the state been cutting our budget, but, because of the failing local economy, our enrollment is declining and there are the inevitable rumors of layoffs. Recently I came to work and the head librarian, who comes to work about half an hour after I do, said first thing as she walked in the door, "You look good, unless you have a job interview or something today."

That reminded me of the following story about my last job, which I told her. Before the job I currently have, a couple of years ago, I was working in a public library in the same town. That library, too, was having financial problems, and everyone knew—it wasn't just rumors—that layoffs were coming. I had already started putting out my resume, and had gotten an interview at a library system in the Ozarks, a pretty conservative area as you can imagine. In preparation for the interview I cut ten or twelve inches off my hair Thursday evening in order to look less like I'd just stumbled out of a Sixties commune and more like a professional librarian, and then went to work Friday; I was taking vacation time the next week in order to go to the interview. The acting head librarian, *who at that moment had my lay off papers on his desk,* saw me with my short hair and grew visibly angry; he asked if I had a job interview scheduled. I looked him square in the eye and told him that I had cut my hair to donate to Locks of Love.

Now, I could get all "lawyerey" and claim I didn't *actually* lie, that I never *denied* I had a job interview, and that I *had* in fact donated my hair to Locks of Love. But I deliberately side-stepped the issue and misled my questioner. And that's honestly the same thing.

So, I can't get through the first **hour** of work, the first **hour** of my day around other people, without simultaneously violating the precept against False Speech and the injunction in favor of Right Speech in the Eightfold Path. But Shinran says Amida really doesn't expect any better than that from me. We are all foolish beings, and fall short on the Path. I can't, or at least shouldn't, hold myself to the standards of the Buddhas. After an evening of discussion with my American elite Buddhist friends I like to return to Shinran and remind myself that there's room in the Pure Land for screw-ups like me, as well.

Namu Amida Butsu.

Gassho

WHAT IS YOUR *REAL* NAME
Andy Jiyo Agacki

Act II Scene II *Romeo and Juliet* by Bill Shakespeare

Juliet:

>O Romeo, Romeo! wherefore art thou Romeo?
>Deny thy father and refuse thy name;
>Or, if thou wilt not, be but sworn my love,
>And I'll no longer be a *Capulet.*

Romeo:

>[Aside] Shall I hear more, or shall I speak at this?

Juliet:

>'Tis but thy name that is my enemy;
>Thou art thyself, though not a Montague.
>What's Montague? it is nor hand, nor foot,
>Nor arm, nor face, nor any other part
>Belonging to a man. O, be some other name!
>What's in a name? that which we call a rose
>By any other name would smell as sweet;
>So Romeo would, were he not Romeo call'd,
>Retain that dear perfection which he owes
>Without that title. Romeo, doff thy name,
>And for that name which is no part of thee
>Take all myself.

Romeo:

>I take thee at thy word:
>Call me but love, and I'll be new baptized;
>Henceforth I never will be Romeo.

Now, I DO like Shakespeare …. Really …. And I mean no offense to the ol' Bard. This famous scene has been a kind of Koan for me … for what IS in a name, anyway?

I've been called a baby (when I *was* one), and teenager, too, an adult (now that I *am*) though I don't think it's true.

Then there's egg-head, debater, director, an actor, too, but not black or yellow or red but *white*, though sometimes I'm blue.

A damned fool, a clown and maverick, too, and a little shit taunted, but did not take the cue.

A business consultant, manager, too, troublemaker, sinner, (to mention a few).

But I am Andrew Stanley Agacki, named after my Dziadzia (that's in Polish to you)

In Korean my Dharma Name is Hae Kwang (Wisdom River) but that's not new.

A Catholic, A UU (that I *am*) and (though I'm not) *proudly* a Jew.

And I still laugh (when on camera) she said, 'Are you Japanese', poor, young soul ... she hadn't a clue.

And now I am humble Jiyo to you, a 'Natural Sun' ... and Lay Minister too.

And so many more of the labels I've had, like Speaker and poet ...

But 'enemy'? No ...

So many labels we take, we are given, in this life. But what IS the *real* you? I joined up in this Dharma business to find my *real* name. And sometimes, in the whispering rustle of forest leaf, or raging explosion of Winter thunder I think I hear it.

But I'm deaf in one ear, so it's not been quite clear.

So my Dharma ear listens, and listens still more ......

What is *YOUR Real Name*?

SOMETIMES THERE ARE NO WORDS
Andy Jiyo Agacki

After Sunday Service is over at our UU church, we all noisily gather in the Common Room for what we jokingly call, our 'Communion Coffee'. Last Sunday was the same. The usual small chit-chat followed over coffee … and then I spied an old friend at a far corner I hadn't seen for a few months.

Something didn't seem right: it was the way she stood, her gestures, more 'puffiness' in her face … I don't know …. Just SOMEthing.

Making my way to her, I then said (cautiously), "Haven't seen you for a while …. How're you doin'?"

"Well," she said, "they cut my hours at work by half in November. A week later, I found out I had cancer, and they took me pretty much right to surgery. 'They couldn't get it all,' they said. They released me a few days later, but then I was back in, because I developed a severe Staph infection. That took even longer in the hospital."

She showed me how much of her thigh had 'disappeared' as a result of the infection. "I start Chemo next week," she finished.

"Uh," I hated to ask, "will this be covered by your insurance?"

"They tell me probably not, since it was discovered only AFTER the insurance was canceled.".

I looked into her eyes, then hugged her tightly. "Anything I can do for you, I said?"

"Maybe you can't think of anything yet," I told her, "least, not until things play out further. Just let me know anything you need help with along the way, Okay?"

"You can chant for me,", she said, smiling.

"Will do … will do," I responded, as she noticed her 'ride' was looking for her to leave.

Afterwards. I felt so inadequate. All these years of practice … hmph. Didn't have much to offer for all that. But as I ruminate on it further, I think … it *was* enough. Sometimes, I've found, there ARE no words ... sometimes only a tear and love comes, and it is all we can give ... and it is … *enough* … I'll chant, though ... I promised her that.

Walk in peace, my friends …. Walk in peace.

IT'S ALL GOOF
John Miyo Wylder

First thing you need to know is, I get migraines. Most of them aren't too bad, but some of them get . . . interesting. With a really bad one, I can actually see sounds. Large dogs bark in a kind of rusty brown color, my wife talks in sort of bluish-tinged silver, a Harley Davidson's exhaust is just black with flecks of brown, in case you were curious. I actually had one migraine so bad I got to see the Virgin Mary appear, kneel down, and pray over me while I was lying on the floor at work.

Second thing you need to know for this story to make sense is that my daughter just started her first year of college, in a small college out-of-state, about three hours from here, and she's going through all the usual what she calls "adult with training wheels" stuff that college kids go through. For instance, she called home four of five times one night to talk to her mother because she was trying to figure out how to do laundry. She'd ask one question, and hang up. Fifteen minutes later, she'd call back, ask her question, get her answer, and hang up. Or the night she called to ask mom if you were supposed to put leftover pizza in the refrigerator or the freezer. I get the calls when her computer's acting up.

These two threads wove together about a month ago when I got a reasonably bad migraine. I couldn't actually *see* sounds, but I could *feel* them rippling through my body in waves. Normally when I go to bed, I set my cell phone to ring loudly enough to wake if someone (my daughter) calls, and set it by the bed, but that night I forgot and left it set to vibrate and in the den to boot. I woke up the next morning feeling fine at my usual time (5:00—I need time to meditate and, let's be honest, watch Youtube videos before work) and saw that she'd called me *four times* between 9:45 and 10:15 that night before giving up. That shows a certain level of panic. I texted her back with an explanation and asked if it was too late to help, and if it was, if she had managed to solve the problem without me. Several worried hours later I got a text back from her assuring me everything was OK; it read simply, "It's all goof."

I *assume* that was a typo for "It's all good," but I don't care. I'll take brilliance wherever I can steal it. I'm not proud.

It's all goof. I tend to take this world so seriously, as if it were important somehow. "Is my boss happy with me?" "Which insurance plan should I sign up for?" "Oh Lord, did you see the election results?" I need to just relax. It's all goof. I keep hearing people say things like, "Let go and let G~d," and it works for them, so that's good, but I've never been able to do that; it just never managed to really register with me. It's just too . . . "Goofy". But "It's all goof" works for me, because now I get to not only take the world lightly, but laugh at it, too. Admit to the humor, the absurdity of it all. The imperfect, unsatisfactory, impermanent, ridiculous nature of all compounded things. When I remember.

It's all goof. I haven't found what I'm looking for yet, but I'm keeping my eyes open for just the right Walt Disney merchandising—I want just the right Bodhisattva Goofy icon for my altar. I'll know it when I see it. I've even got this image in my head of Goofy in saffron robes sitting on a lotus blossom that might make a nice tattoo. I'll have to sit with that one for a while.

It's all goof. It doesn't have the depth of "Form is emptiness; emptiness is form," but as someone who approaches the great depth of Dharma wisdom only to run back to the kiddie pool, I'm happy with it. When I get hung up on making the Right Decision To Avoid Dire Consequences (all caps, like in Winnie the Pooh), which I frequently do, I repeat my new mantra, "It's all goof," and somehow it all seems a bit sillier, A Bit Less Important (again, all in caps).

It's all goof.
Gassho.

GEORGE THE LIPOMA
Andy Jiyo Agacki

Had an interesting day about a week-and-a-half ago, despite the surgeon's comments.

I had a decades old lipoma removed from my shoulder. If you must know, a lipoma is a benign tumor composed of adipose tissue (which is just a fancy name for body fat). I just called it 'George', since we had been friends for so long.

Doctors always told me, 'Don't pay any mind to it, but if it grows, or gives you trouble, then we'll look at it'. A few weeks ago, George got all up and angry; swelling up and hurting. Time to see what made him so cranky. The ultra-sound was 'inconclusive', but I *did* determine it was a boy. Isn't that what ultra-sounds are for, to determine the sex and condition of your baby? The nurse and I had fun with that, hence the name 'George'.

Hemming and hawing, the surgeon and I decided George might as well go; never know when that little guy would get angry again.

The surgery was a local-anesthetic, out-patient procedure. Probably 20 minutes of all of us (4 others plus myself and the surgeon) laughing and carrying on. There *were* some *ouch* moments, though. Surgeon said they should have used a general anesthetic because he had to go in a lot deeper than he anticipated.

Poor George went to pieces under the surgeon's scalpel. He was just too deeply entrenched to give up without a fight.

Surgeon also said It wasn't the most interesting surgery he'd ever done, but, 'It sure was the funniest', he laughed! Guess being a disorderly orderly for almost the whole of the 1970's figured in on our little surgical comedy.

It was my first ever surgery of any kind.

A dear friend of mine wasn't quite so lucky. What was diagnosed by his family doctor as 'merely' another lipoma, led to a removal of a cancer ridden muscle in his leg. His prognosis is good … still …

You just 'don't know'.

And that 'don't know' leads me to cogitating a bit ….

I find myself ruminating over that koan I call 'The Great Matter' more as the moments, days and years progress. I always wondered if, as I got older, I'd start to get more agitated about illnesses and the ever impending 'doom'.

Seems the direction of my thoughts lead me to pick up those little bits of stone and rubble I'm finding along the way; rubbing my thumbs on them to get the dirt off, jostling them around in my hand, admiring those little things right by my feet.

Oh, death's there: with her long scythe and all (though her long, hooded gown is a bit more fashionable and not so 'Goth' as she's usually pictured), and we sit down and chat whenever she's in the area ... like that day in surgery. We, Death and I, like to keep in touch, knowing there'll be the usual 'business' further down the road, but it's fine chatting just the same, sometimes about a Funeral or Memorial Service I have to officiate (she gives me some pointers on what to say). But no, there's just too much to see and pay attention to while these moments pass under my shoes.

Death is only a *part* of the Great Matter:

Life is the other part.

Death is a certainty full of unknowns answered only *after* we die.

Life is an uncertainty full of change, possibility and answers *right here and now while we're living*

Don't waste your time with Death's final walk. Talk to her now and then to get the *feel* of her business, but don't dwell on something she's really not going to answer until that final moment.

Take the time given to you in the here and now of life, in the people and things around you *right now*.

That biopsy of mine? Still don't know the results, despite all the assurances of a 'benign' encounter. And my reaction to it is not that 'agitation' I wondered about having, earlier, instead, I find it's a greater *intimacy*. Koyo Sensei suggested as much to me a few days ago. I think that word works just fine. And yet ...

In the words of that great philosopher, Yogi Berra, 'It ain't over till it's over'. But still ....

It's beautiful, this time of year!

Arigato!

Thank you.

WAVES
Ricardo Ryuyo Sasaki

Last week I spent 5 days in the beautiful beaches of Recife, in northeast Brazil (I live in the Southeast). All days spending at the beaches, lots of sun, clean sands. I got a terrific price on a flight so I got two tickets, for me and my son, and away we went. I took the chance and also gave three talks on Buddhism & meditation there. Overall, it was a great experience. Though I was born in a coast city, where I live now is surrounded by mountains and everyone complains there is no ocean near here. So going to the coast is really pleasant. And there I was, sitting at the beach, thinking about what I was going to say about meditation to people that night. The answer was right in front of me. Thich Nhat Hanh talks about waves and sea in the book we are reading at the Lay Program. How individual waves think they are individual, deluding themselves in forgetfulness that all ARE just water. However I made another turn in the symbol of sea and waves. I was thinking about a possible connection to meditation, since that was the subject I was going to talk about. And it occurred to me it had the two elements essential in Buddhist meditation. What in Theravada tradition is called samatha-vipassana, the Chinese used to call chih-kuan. I always loved the way they translated it: *Stop and See*.

So the first move in our meditation practice is Stop. We need to calm down, concentrate, focus our mind in whatever object we choose to use. In my case, body sensations and breathing. I look at the sea and observe the beautiful vastness of it. The waves give rhythm, and their coming and going relax us, calming us down through its soothing magic. Like in the breathing, watching its coming and going, looking at the waves also gives us that relaxing effect. And facing the vastness of the sea opens a space inside, empty and pure, and at the same time, a fulfilling space. It is like the inner space we need to create while meditating. Breathing in, breathing out, calming down, creating space. Clouds come and go, the space remains. Waves come and go, the ocean remains.

The other aspect of meditation is vipassana, what the Chinese call Seeing. Seeing what? We can say seeing the inner truth, the reality of what things really are, something Thich Nhat Hanh always talks about a lot. In Theravada tradition, vipassana is seeing with the eyes of impermanence, unsatisfactoriness and no-self. We need to see our experience with that perspective. And again the waves give such an example for that! Their coming and going, ups and downs show us that things arise and pass away. What is now is not in the following moment. "*Am I the boy of eighteen in the photograph*", asks Thich Nhat Hanh, or "*the old man of seventy?*". Or none of them? No-self is clear when watching the waves. Try to catch a wave! You can´t. Try catch it, and you get frustrated, stressed. You suffer trying to make the reality something it is not. So during five days, my son and I spent being calm and cool watching the sea, and riding the waves of impermanence, unsatisfactoriness and no-self, enjoying the waves, going with them, without foolishly trying to catch them. I look at my shorts and read the brand name of it: "Waverider". Thank you.

POWER OUTAGE
Andy Jiyo Agacki

I was recording my Dharma talk after the power went out about 15 minutes before I started. It was an off-the-cuff talk, since that loss of power caused me to cogitate on the matter. What I had written to present just didn't seem important anymore.

Then, as I was getting to the end of my talk, ready to 'wrap up'—the power went out. Now, since I have everything on cable, that meant the phones, too.

Did I pay my bill? Didn't think that was the problem.

I rent a flat in a building over 100 years old, and it's gone out before.

So I called WE Energies (on my cell phone), and got a recorded message, "We have an extremely high volume of calls … Please call back later," just as I stepped outside to some pretty blustery winds to find that even the stop and go lights were off up the block.

Adrienne Sensei had called me on my cell, and we'd rescheduled for a couple of hours later (to *now*).

I hoped everything would be back up by then.

What a tenuous thing our lives are.

There was a big solar flare last week. I wondered about that: No, the effects of it would have dissipated by now. But I remember reading this past summer about a solar flare that was big enough to pass the earth's orbit. The report said not to worry—we weren't there! Hmm.

The odds are overwhelming, I've read, that the earth will be struck by an asteroid big enough to cause major damage—not in our lifetime, maybe, but one of those things has our space address on it, nonetheless.

There's also a huge magma pocket set to blow in Yellowstone National Park—it seems we're 'overdue' on that. That eruption will be devastating for up to 1,000 miles.

What a tenuous thing our lives are.

And what are we doing with our precious time? We're paying bills, surfing the web, arguing, fighting, killing: Living our lives and not living, polluting the air, the water and dying.

I had my sixth-month checkup at the doctor's not that many months ago. My posts on Facebook read:

I have my 6 month checkup in about 11 hrs.
I am 3 score and 3 years.
I am dying.
We are ALL dying.

If you do not grasp this ....
You are just dying ...
Please live ...
Okay?

And after the appointment:

6 month checkup with new doctor.
Talked about still being
- Vertical
- Breathing
- Mobile
And how age bends the boundaries a mite
(Now and then).
Death only poked her head in
To say, 'Hi!
So many deadlines lately ...'
(In apology).
But time enough to brush cheeks
(Time enough).

So now, right now .... What are you doing? What is your *job*?
Your *real* job?
Please grasp this
Otherwise we are just dying
Please LIVE!
Okay?

Peace ... and thank you.

LAY MINISTER CLASS #2

5 WAYS HOW NOT TO BE
A BODHISATTVA AND OTHER CONFESSIONS OF
A DHARMA PRACTITIONER
Wendy Shinyo Haylett

1) I thought if I became a Buddhist it would profoundly change me and I would get all spiritual ... better ... different ... then I would change the world.

Becoming a Buddhist did NOT profoundly change me. Studying the Dharma did NOT profoundly change me, directly. Imitating practitioners doing Buddhist practices did NOT profoundly change me.

But I was profoundly changed by "looking carefully" as Rev. Gyomay Kubose wrote, and finding the truth of things as they are, of suchness—finding universal life "deeply within [myself and in all things around me." He wrote "To learn Buddhism is to become aware of life, which means to become aware of oneself."

I am profoundly changed by not becoming different or more spiritual, but becoming intimate with who I am, in all my foolish, ego grasping, judging thoughts. In that intimacy, I learned to develop compassion for myself for being this foolish being, which creates space to change a bit by not blindly acting on the foolish thoughts. And, with compassion for myself, compassion for others increased, because I saw how we were the same in our foolishness.

2) I thought if I studied ALL the Buddhist texts I would become wise.

I studied the Lam Rim, the Prajnaparamita, Buddhist epistomology and Buddhist logic, the Abidharma, Madhyamika philosophy, the Vinaya, Lojong, The Way of the Bodhisattva, Nagarjuna's Seventy Stanzas, and on and on.

Although I learned much that I have been able to take inside and examine in my life, I did not become wise. I became wiser when I tried to apply what I learned and watched how my mind worked, with no "rigid expectancies and no self-conscious intentions", as Rev. Gyomay wrote.

Rev. Gyomay wrote, "To learn Buddhism is to change one's life. Regardless of how much we learn, unless your life changes, nothing is learned—it is just accumulated knowledge." He also wrote "When there is too much 'mind' in our activities we become artificial and our lives do not flow smoothly. Life must flow out from within and not for external reasons."

I'll still study, meditate on, and refer to the texts of the masters, but not to become wise. Not to become anybody, but to better understand myself. And in understanding myself, my need to become anything has lessened, because I see that I already am. In the confidence of being what I already am, I can genuinely meet and be with all others—with no desire to be more wise. Maybe that's wise and maybe it's foolish, but I know it's things as they are.

3) I thought if I met a great teacher or Lama and get a Dharma name, my being would somehow be altered and I would cease to be my old stupid self.

I met and took teachings from a lot of wonderful teachers, some of who may be enlightened. I am also the proud "owner" of four Dharma names:

I am Tenzin Chödron, or "Dharma Lamp of the Teachings", my first ordination name received by Venerable Drupon Jorphel Rinpoche, a Drikung Kagyu Lama, who proclaimed that now my life would have meaning.

I am Könchog Zangmo, or "Noble Triple Gem", ordained by His Eminence Garchen Rinpoche, also a Drikung Kagyu Lama, who is respected by many lamas as a pure and realized master.

I am Könchog Pema, "Three Jewels Lotus", ordained by Venerable Khenpo Sherab Özer Rinpoche, a Drikung Kagyu Lama and accomplished scholar who exudes love.

I am Shinyo, "Heart Sun", through my Tisarana with Koyo Kubose Sensei, a meeting with a teacher given to me by the loving and compassionate grace of Amida's light, of life. I did not seek this teacher, but the teachings called to me.

Each teacher did alter me somehow. A little seed was planted by each. And each name pointed me toward the truth. Each name, a signpost pointing toward where I needed to go:

Tenzin Chödron: Dharma Lamp of the Teachings … a bit of rebel name for within the Drikung Kagyu lineage, pointing to where I had come from: from some years studying Gelupa teachings through the Asian Classics Institute. Pointed me toward continued study and to hold the Dharma as my compass, my rock.

Könchog Zangmo: Noble Triple Gem. The Könchog, or triple gem part, is the lineage name, which I also share with Sayo Sensei. The Noble part tripped me up when I first received it, puffing me up at the thought of getting the name Noble—a wonderful teacher, indeed, Garchen Rinpoche. The challenge to me was to see what that meant. And it wasn't about me.

Könchog Pema: My Bodhisattva name, given when taking the Bodhisattva vows. Again the lineage name of Könchog, or the Three Jewels, but then Pema, the lotus. The perfect signpost to begin on the path of the Bodhisattva. It's all about being in the muddy pond with the whole world … or even just your neighbor. You can't work as a Bodhisattva without getting a little muddy.

Shinyo: And of course Shinyo, Heart Sun. Kokoro, as Rev. Koyo explained to me, has many meanings: essentially heart, mind, or center/essence. When Rev. Koyo gave me the name, he mentioned a warm heart. This has been the path of the Dharma revealed to me by Bright Dawn: the heart-mind, not just the mind. Rowing with both oars—wisdom and compassion to get to the essence of the Dharma, the essence of myself.

Each teacher, each name, planted the seeds. But I had to water the seed and make sure it was planted in good soil, had plenty of water and sun, and to continue to tend the sprout so as not to be choked by weeds or eaten by insects. Teachers can plant seeds in us, but we have a choice whether to nurture them or let it die. To live the truth they teach and model to us.

Gyomay Kubose Sensei wrote "Unless we are aware, we do not learn anything. We have inspiration and no teachings. Teachings are everywhere—all around us—if only we open the mind's eye to see."

I haven't ceased to be my old stupid self, I am Wendy Shinyo now, and taking that name as my guidance keeps me pointed in the right direction, to the heart of who I am. That name enabled me to embrace my bombu nature, as the heart or source of wisdom and compassion. As Rev. Gyomay wrote, "We have to be ourselves.... Each of us is unique and perfect."

4) *I thought that if I studied and practiced to become a teacher or minister, only then would I have the qualifications to help the world by spreading the Dharma. I thought that becoming a teacher would make me better.*

It wasn't long after I realized that becoming a Buddhist wasn't going to make everything different, then I had the thought that studying all the Buddhist texts might be the ticket. Soon after I knocked off 18 courses through the Asian Classics Institute, and saw that my life hadn't profoundly changed, then I thought that it must be taking refuge and getting Ordained and a new Dharma name. Then after taking teachings and getting empowerments from one teacher, and saw that I hadn't changed that much for the better, and was no closer to enlightenment, I thought I must need to connect with another teacher—maybe my heart teacher—and get a new teaching for things to change.

And then, even though I found what I felt was the true teaching and my life DID begin to change, I thought I was still not quite ready to share what I knew—somehow not made of the right stuff—or not possessing the right credentials. Maybe another course, maybe another title, maybe… maybe...

But, as Rev. Gyomay Kubose wrote, in our culture it's all about purpose and goal-orientation. He said purposeless action is considered meaningless. Yet, he stressed, in addition to purposefulness, the other side of life is purposelessness. "Both aspects are true," he wrote. To accomplish things we must have purpose, but there is purposelessness too. "A flower blooms, a bird sings, a child plays..." The flower cannot help but bloom as it does—there is no intention. Water flows effortlessly.... When you love, you love."

Sensei wrote, "If we do something from the beginning with purpose and meaning, then it becomes quite rigid. Meaning and reasons may be given later but the doing is the purpose itself. If we continually live in the midst of purposeful, directed activity, soon we feel pressured and "must" enters our lives. There is no naturalness.... Buddha taught that the essence of life just is, as it is.... If we analyze it, it becomes two, but the reality is always one.... Only when we analyze do we have different directions. True reality is natural and purposeless.... When one just is, one forgets all other things, ones forgets self." Sensei quotes Dogen,"To know oneself is to forget oneself" and he adds: "One just is."

5) *I thought I could help the world by spreading the Dharma through teaching, blogs, and writing ... if only I had hours of time each day to devote to nothing else but that. I thought everyday life was preventing me from spiritual realization. I thought the people in my life were somehow not the "all beings" I vowed to save.*

Yep, it's always something ... you sit down to meditate and the dog needs to go out ... You were going to write that Dharma talk and you need to go to your mother-in-law's house to fix the TV ... you pop in your ear pods to listen to a talk you've been waiting to hear for weeks and your neighbor runs up behind you and asks to walk the block with you ... you save the evening to write a blog and your partner begs you to watch a movie with her.

Man, if these people wouldn't keep delaying me, maybe I could do my Bodhisattva work!!

Rev. Gyomay Sensei wrote that the "purpose in Buddhism is to overcome the self, overcome the duality of things, overcome multiplicity and become one's true self." He said that "one should become totally selfless" and went on to talk about how a half-full bottle of water makes noise when you shake it, but if it is completely full, there is no air space and no noise. And when the bottle is completely empty there is no noise, because there is no water. He taught that selflessness is when we are filled to the top and then you become selfless.

He writes, "You should attain complete fullness" and that this is Buddhist selflessness. He says, "You are the one who occupies the whole world.... There is no small, petty self to be disturbed. Even if you are shaken, there is no noise.... Forget enlightenment" he writes. "Forget Buddha.... You become one with the whole universe. This is enlightenment; this is selflessness."

And I will leave you with the same thing as stated in the Prajnaparamita Vajracchedika Sutra (The Diamond Cutter or The Diamond that Cuts through Illusion). In the dialogue between Subhuti and the Buddha, Subhuti asks how to create the most awakened mind. The Buddha answers that no matter how many species of beings there are, that when we lead them all to liberation—to Nirvana or the Pure Land—in fact, when an infinite number have been liberated, there will not be a single being who is liberated, if we are thinking with an enlightened mind.

May it be so. Namo Amida Butsu.

BEGOING
David Teiyo Pangburn Jr.

Gyomay Sensei tells us that "life is becoming". My focus is on this "becoming" and it occurs in each moment. While pondering this truth, I developed my own term, perhaps because of my dualism, but maybe also because of my insight. That term is "be-going". For I find that there is life in each moment that is 'becoming.' I have come to see that the connection each moment has with impermanence makes each moment a 'be-going' too.

Why do I have all this Dr Suess language? Basically, because I am alive. The Buddha first noticed "life is suffering." Walking upright and about in this world will cause you to notice this fact of suffering. A good friend had a stroke this past month. She is 53 years old. Her husband has phoned me a couple times to give me updates, and empty out his pain. She is home now, but unable to communicate, and her right arm is paralyzed. She can move about, but there are issues with her bowels, and she is totally frustrated in adapting to her new lifestyle. Her husband feels lost. He is finding out what the role of care giver involves, and like any of us, he is not prepared for what has come his way. You never stop to think about what impermanence could entail.

Life involves becoming but at the same time it involves be-going. We observe a flower… it grows, develops, opens, and becomes a thing of beauty, but it does not stop there. The complete cycle of life includes optimal growth followed by demise. The flower soon turns brown, shrivels, collapses, and joins the earth. It has to do this to live completely.

I am at an age where I am observing the demise of many of my peers, as well as my parents, their parents… and I am realizing that I too, am in the autumn of my life. Actually, many flowers don't make it to full bloom: accidents and insects cut them off before they achieve their full potential. We lucky flowers get to bloom and the whole world is watching; but even the most beautiful flowers must grow full cycle.

So I can accept my "be-going" while I am becoming. I hope my understanding of this becomes much clearer as I age, so I can help those along who wrestle with the be-going issue. It's all One. I am happy to embrace impermanence as a full realization of my potential. When I reach the day of leaving I hope my beauty was a wonderful experience for many, and I also hope my demise may be a lesson in completing the life cycle as a part of full potential.

Are we to rise above suffering? Are we to wallow in it? Suffering comes in many forms, but whatever way it comes it is a part of our inner being that comes across as suffering. It's there, it's a simple fact of living, and the Buddha told us to let go of it when it reveals itself to us. Gyomay Sensei reminded us that non-attachment is not detachment. We feel. Suffering is an experience. We can transcend it. It is one side of the experience. We must come full circle. Living life to its fullest demands that we go full circle, and we can rest assured that we will be alright.

DAUGHTER'S GRADUATION
Kenneth Muyo Swanson

We were on the college campus a few weeks ago, driving to our daughter's college Baccalaureate service. I was in a hurry, even though we were not late or pressed for time. A young man on a bicycle in front of us was moseying down the middle of the street. I blew my horn for him to pull over and let us pass. He signaled a left turn and then immediately flipped me the finger. As both of us turned left, I accelerated and pulled alongside of him, rolled down the window and yelled at him, "Would you like to stop and I'll get out and you can do that again to my face?" Jennifer whacked me on the arm to stop it. The young man said something unkind about my carbon footprint and drove off. Jennifer said to me, "Chill! He's a kid on a bike, and you're in an SUV. He signaled his turn, give him a break." And then, "What kind of Buddhist are you?"

Well, I've been thinking of that. Clearly, at that moment, I was not practicing the vows of the four noble disciplines of patience. The four Dharmas are to be patient and,

1) not respond to anger with anger,
2) not respond to physical harm with physical harm,
3) not respond to criticism with criticism, and,
4) not respond to verbal argument with verbal argument.

These four noble disciplines are said to distinguish a real practitioner, as they refer to the causes of anger and lack of patience. If you retaliate in any of the four circumstances, you are breaking this branch vow.

I've got a ways to go. Will I ever get to the point where I can fulfill the vows that I make? Do I have the right vows? Are there vows that I can take that are easier to fulfill and then, later, I can make graduated vows? It made me start thinking about vows in general and more specific. I write down some ideas, but they seemed long and impossible. Then I think, what's the point? I might as well stop, maybe I'm not cut out for this. I can't undo what has been done. But, maybe I can redeem myself -- if I am sincere and express my regret, can I, at least, prevent more negative karma from happening?

When we returned from Graduation Weekend, Rainer Maria Rilke informed me (through my Zen Calendar quote for the day) to chill. (Again!):

I would like to beg you, dear sir, to have patience with everything unresolved in your heart and to try to love the questions themselves as if they were locked rooms or books written in a very foreign language. Don't search for the answers, which could not be given to you now, because you would not be able to live them. And the point is, to live everything. Live the questions now. Perhaps then, some day in the far future, you will gradually, without even noticing it, live your way into the answer.

So maybe I'm trying too hard right now to figure it out. I look at the advice that Koyo Sensei gives on many occasions and has served him pretty well in his life and travels: "Keep Going."

That's what I intend to do.

WHERE'S WALDO?
Wendy Shinyo Haylett

I remember thinking about the first few Dharma Glimpses I was assigned to in my first year in the Bright Dawn Lay Ministry training program. I would feel anxious in a search to find the "perfect" something that was appropriate as a subject for a Dharma Glimpse.

But that is the point of glimpses: Not to search, but to keep our eyes open. The Dharma is teaching every minute, everywhere, but we're too busy reading, or looking for it, to see it. Like the *Where's Waldo* books or those Facebook posts that ask whether you see two faces or a vase. Things are the way they are – to us – based on what we're looking for and how open we are to seeing what's there.

That reminds me of a crow experience I had. I was sitting on the porch, working on my laptop, not paying attention to what was happening in the yard. Some movement caught my eye as it interrupted the beam of sunlight. I quickly glanced, then went into alarm mode when my brain interpreted what were 4 or 5 crows walking in the yard as two black dogs running towards me.

For a few seconds, the crows WERE black dogs running towards me. That was my experience. It was as real as the crows the dogs became, when I really focused on them. Like dreams, the stuff in our world is up for interpretation.

And each individual's interpretation is colored by a complex web of causes and conditions that we cannot know about in the other or about ourselves. As the *Buddhism Boot Camp* author, Tiber Hawkeye, says, "the opposite of what you know is also true."

Which is another way of saying, "Things are not as they seem, nor are they otherwise," which is an email signature line I use from the *Lankavatara Sutra*.

If you only see a crow walking, then you are trapped in the linear, conceptual, dual perspective of the world as either-or and the non-dual perspective of mystics, believers in a spiritual or transcendent realm, artists, poets, writers, engineers, inventors, scientists, and mathematicians will be blocked to you. You will miss the actual door to heaven, while you are attending the lecture on how to get there.

It is written that Michelangelo stared at a block of marble for four months. Is it because he was "conceiving" what to turn it into, or rather, was he divining what it ALREADY MUST BE?

In writing class we are cautioned to show not tell, which means going beyond labels to just be with an experience or setting just as it is. The world would be pretty dull and nothing new would be invented—no art, no novels or stories—if we stuck to what we already know, have a name for, or learned in a book. I've seen insects I had never seen before. Do I deny that they exist because I don't have a name or label for them????

And this all brings me back around to remembering my father, this Father's Day, who passed away in March of 2006. My father was a great teacher to me, and not in the way you expect me to tell you about right now. He was a great father who loved and respected his four kids, encouraged us in our dreams, wanted the best for us, worked hard to give us the best of everything, which he did, and never said no to us when we asked for anything.

Yet, the biggest and best lesson I learned from my Dad is that "things are not as they seem, nor are they otherwise." He taught me the *Lankavatara Sutra* through his struggles with bipolar mental illness. My Dad's bipolar condition mostly manifested as mania, so he was very present all the time and the biggest energy in any room.

In the essay tribute I wrote for his obituary, titled *Beautiful Mind: Big Ideas*, I borrowed the title from Sylvia Nasar's biography of the mathematical genius and Nobel Laureate, John Nash. John Nash saw the world differently than others, because he struggled with delusions caused by schizophrenia. My Dad, too, saw the world differently through the perspective of bipolar disease.

A day before my dad's death, his grandson, Dan, said "I think he is why I have so many big ideas." These words describe my Dad perfectly. He lived in the realm of big ideas. And those of us who received one of his frequent phone calls or visits heard plenty of those ideas up until the last few days of his life. My dad was brilliant. He was also different. Yet many or most would have labeled him as crazy or insane, after talking to him during one of his unmedicated periods.

Yet, as the years went by, I learned that no matter how crazy it seemed to rake snow, or that he claimed for years there were electrical waves running though his apartment coming from some special device the scientist son of his neighbor designed and installed just to torture him, it didn't make it not true. To him.

And I learned to nod in agreement or even ask questions about the wedding being planned: The one of him, the 87-year-old man in the nursing home to the 30-year old nurse.

Yet my Dad at the same time was tender-hearted and brilliant and that was also true. Once we label something as crazy, or crow, or black dogs, we have stopped the possibility for it to be anything else, because we immediately begin responding to the person or thing as labeled.

So where can we "glimpse" the Dharma? And where do we find Buddha? Or God? We COULD find the Dharma in a book, or the Buddha in a temple, or God in a church. But it's more possible that we will find whatever it is we're looking for right where we are. In our own minds, hearts, yards, and neighborhoods. We can see Buddha or God in the faces of our family, dogs, cats, friends, neighbors, and co-workers.

But if your head is full of concepts of what the Dharma is, who Buddha is, who God is, or what is the Absolute, transcendent, divine, or boundless, infinite light of great compassion and wisdom ... then remember "not this, not this." It is not this, nor is it that.

It is only when you release your life and the people in it, and the world around you, from the shackles of what they have already been labeled, that you will see the Dharma. If you could see everything from that space for even 10 minutes, everything around you will sing the Dharma.

Happy Father's Day and, as Rev. Koyo says, "Have a Buddha-Full Day!

LIFE EVENTS
David Teiyo Pangburn, Jr.

This Glimpse is a cornucopia of recent life events. The first event I wanted to write about was a moment I had with one of my colleagues where I work. I found myself enthralled by what was coming out of my mouth during our conversation. We were discussing how everything around us seems to be chaotic during the course of a regular day at our facility. I found myself telling him about living life from within and not allowing external distractions to dictate response and reaction. Our conversation became a mini-Dharma talk as I related some of the recent teachings I had received, although I did not present them as such, but rather it came across like plain common sense. I knew the reason I was able to share this insight was because it has become a reality within me.

My cohort was open to what I was saying and expressed hope that several of the points I made would be helpful to him. What I realized from this moment was that a Dharma talk does not have to be prepared in advance. A Dharma talk can be a part of a normal conversation, mostly because Dharma is a part of who we are and it will flow in all aspects of our lives…how we perceive life situations, how we discuss them, how we experience them, how we live our life!

The second event that has been taking place in my life relates to anger issues. I have been struggling with anger at my workplace. I am not an angry type guy. I am pretty laid back in my approach to life and I do not get upset very quickly. I try to maintain a good sense of humor in my approach to everyday living. Part of growing as a Buddhist includes learning how to address the external disruptions caused by others.

Just because I am trying to live a peaceful and focused life does not mean that everyone else is also doing the same. I seem to frequently encounter others who are living life frantically and are oblivious to being considerate of others. (Been there, done that myself a few times!) I try very hard to look past the foibles of the unenlightened. I do not stand in judgment of folks, because they are, in reality, a part of me in the overall scheme of life and, if I judge you, I am judging myself. But it is so easy to become annoyed when someone is not compassionate with others.

I see mean-spirited actions every day, not only among our consumers, (who are mentally ill), but between staff members. I would like to stand in place in a non-dualistic way while the darts are thrown around me, but oh! How difficult! Some of this involves immoral relations between supervisors and other staff members which casts a pall over the other staff members. It puts us in a position that is totally uncomfortable. I am not sure how to be a "good Buddhist" in the face of an ugly situation. Some co-workers have inquired if I have a Buddhist viewpoint over the way some things are done both professionally and personally. I want to answer "mu".

Finally, I keep thinking about the monk who carried the girl through the water. Am I living like that monk or am I living like his attendant? If I have to carry the girl through the water day after day, is it still only this moment that I have to think about? Dukha keeps on coming along with the dharma. To muddle through each day requires awareness and the ability to make the right choices. Right choices come from the eightfold path, not from our mental constructs.

ANTS AND WORMS
Paul Toyo Mack

It's been hell-hot here for a week, with no rain, and the a/c still on. *Whew*!

I walk my dog Louie twice a day, in the morning when it's still only in the high 70s and in the early evening, with temps in the high 80s or low 90s. When it's hot but dry, I'm reminded of the high Texas or Moroccan desert.
When it's hot and humid, I'm reminded I'm in Saint Louis!

More and more on my walks with Louie, I'm seeing unfortunate victims of the heat, along with fortunate beneficiaries, playing out life's struggles on a small scale (small to me, though surely titanic to them).

As earthworms seek moisture to ply their trade (the soil is now dry down to five feet here), they crawl out and seek to cross the vast sidewalk on their quest. Many succumb to the heat pounding down and pulsing up, and never quite make it from grassy verge to grassy verge.

I wonder how the ants know there is a juicy morsel waiting to be overwhelmed? Are there ant scouts? Do worms holler for help, only to summon diners?

For me, though it's sad to see ants surrounding a moribund worm and descending on it. (But should ants wait respectfully for the worm's passing and its rapid desiccation? They crave moisture, too.)

I do understand that that's how life is. As the Spanish expression has it, *es parte del paseo*, that is, it's part of life's journey.

WATER
Ken Muyo Swanson

I was looking out the window the other day and saw the blue heated water bowl—a bright island in the middle of the snow. Every day of the year, we put out fresh water in two areas for the birds and wildlife. In the next few weeks, our ducks will return. Each year, they fly in around the Ides of March (March 15) and stay with us until Mid-July. Our small city lot can have as many as a dozen ducks gathered for corn and water. Twice a day, I have to clean their bowl and pour fresh water. I enjoy this "chore." I'm looking forward to their arrival. Sometimes they fly in and see everything covered with snow. Then, they fly away and return in a week or so, when they see "their" bowl and the feed on the ground.

I always took water for granted, growing up. Living on Lake Michigan, water was always plentiful and near. My Grandfather and uncles cut ice from the river in winter. I lived with an aunt every summer on a spring-fed lake, and swam in the cold water.

I read what Dogen said about water:

> *Water is neither strong nor weak, neither wet not dry, neither moving nor still, neither cold nor hot, neither being nor non-being, neither delusion nor enlightenment. Solidified, it is harder than diamond: who could break it? When melted, it is softer than milk: who could break it? This being so, how can we doubt the many virtues realized by water?*

Studying water reminds us of the study of our self. We, too, can be flexible like water, adjusting to our environments. Water has no fixed characteristic. There is no one way to see or describe it. I think that is just like we are.

I'd like to be more mindful of water in my life. I have a small bowl that I've filled with water, and put it on the table by my Buddha in the front window. The level of the water in the bowl depends on my attention to it. If I don't refill it, it will go dry. If I fill it too much, it overflows. Isn't that just like our Dharma practice. If we neglect our practice, it dies. If we try too hard, we drown ourselves.

The great tradition of all Buddhas speaks to us in the realm of silence, water and peace. May the true compassion in all our hearts awake to spread good will towards all life everywhere.

May it be so.

APPLE PICKING CORN MAZE
Dave Nichiyo Abatangelo

I took my boys apple picking last week. We go almost every year and for the last three or four years we've been going to an Orchard about an hour away from Chicago. It is a large, very commercial Orchard where you can pick apples and pumpkins, roast hot dogs on an open fire, get homemade apple cinnamon donuts hot out of the fryer and take hay rides. But, for us, the corn maze is really the primary attraction of the farm.

The maze covers a couple of acres and when we do the maze, we typically grab one map apiece. The boys and I then jostle for position as leader of the expedition; each of us wanting to go different ways, lead the charge and have the others follow. This often entails a great deal of negotiation so that we all feel like equal participants in the endeavor. It also involves my wife telling me to relax every time the boys take a turn that I don't think is going to lead us to the next agreed upon checkpoint. She is full of more Buddhist wisdom than she is willing to admit. .

This year we were thrown a curve ball when we were given a single map for the whole group to share. To my surprise, the boys quickly decided that the younger one, Conal, would navigate--with Casimir completely content to follow. Conal lead us quickly from one checkpoint to the next, always cognizant of our current location. About halfway through, Casimir decided that he was bored just following Conal as he tracked to the map. Casimir wanted us to just go through the maze and follow it to wherever it took us. We all agreed on this plan (or in my mind the lack thereof) and started exploring the maze.

As we were walking through the maze, it gradually became apparent that we were being closely followed by a group of kids about the same ages as the boys. It became obvious that not only were they following us but following us was their primary intent. Now, I wasn't sure why they were following us as they didn't know where we were headed. They certainly didn't know that we had decided not to follow the map. We were just following the maze. But, they were following us and said as much. Well, someone saying that they are following a ten year old and twelve year old is tantamount to an explicit challenge. They might as well have said, "We're following you and you can't do anything about it" because we instantly picked up our pace. The kids behind us picked theirs up as well to keep in lock step with us. And shortly the game was afoot!

At the next sharp turn we took off, making a series of quick sudden turns through the maze until we were fully out of sight of our pursuers. We had shaken them. Once we had done that, we slowed down and started walking until we wove our way out. We all agreed that this had been a fun way to explore the maze.

The adventure reminded me of a quote by Lewis Carroll in Alice's Adventures in Wonderland—"If you don't know where you are going, any road will get you there." I often hear this at work when someone charges ahead to do something without really thinking about it. But, as I think about it—especially in context of the maze—not knowing where you are going is a wonderful thing—especially if getting there is your only care. While we were looking to go from checkpoint to checkpoint, I had found it hard to just let Conal lead us. It wasn't until he had proven himself competent at navigating the maze that I was able to let myself just follow him. However, when we decided to roam aimlessly, the means became the end and every step was a right step. I didn't have to worry about whether Conal would get us there—we were there. I've developed a code phrase coming out of this experience. Whenever we take a trip we play a game where the boys ask, "are we there?" They used to ask this about halfway through trip not really knowing how close we are. I would always say, "not yet," or "no, but we're five minutes closer than the last time you asked." Now they jokingly ask if we're there five minutes after leaving the house. I think that my answer from now on will be, "yes, we're there! Of course we're there!"

HUNTING THE GREAT AWAKENED ELEPHANT
Wendy Shinyo Haylett

Dedication to a spiritual path is a treacherous activity, and dedication to a path as a Dharma teacher is ever more treacherous. The innate hazards of attaching to our egos and our self-power as our refuge is ever-present and proportionate to our desire to attain the "end" we have set our sights on...whatever that "end" may be: Dedicated practitioner, teacher, Enlightenment, rebirth in the Pure Land...or whatever.

In the past two months I've been involved in two activities for the Bright Dawn Center: One was researching and writing an article about Rev. Gyomay Kubose, Rev. Koyo Kubose, and the Bright Dawn Center of Oneness Buddhism, which recently published in the Amida Order journal, *Running Tide*. The other was facilitating a sutra study module for the Lay Ministry 6 Class of 2014, focusing on the *Tan Butsu Ge* and *The Heart Sutra* translations and commentaries by Rev. Gyomay Kubose.

I have been immersed in the spiritual, philosophical, and teaching history of our Bright Dawn lineage, rereading teachings, exploring lineage teachers, listening to Dharma talks, and...well, something wonderful has happened. I know Rev. Koyo Kubose's saying is "the Dharma is my rock," but what I have recently experienced is more of the feeling of floating. Immersed in our lineage teachings, I found myself suddenly more buoyant in life, in all aspects of my life. Not like a rock anchoring me, but a natural ability to float. Not a drowning in the details of life, but a floating above.

I felt like I had become one with me, for the first time in many years—like I was naturally me. I began enjoying every part of my life. I was floating through work, through stress, through chores—even through the endless snow-shoveling and cold of the winter of our discontent. I wasn't worried about what I should be doing or how I should be acting. I was just living my life, being with my friends, family, co-workers, and clients, but feeling more authentically myself, connected to a natural flow in everything I did, and at ease.

Everything seemed so natural, so free. It reminded me of a Dharma song that first captivated me some 25 years ago when I was studying and practicing in the Tibetan Buddhist tradition. It is called Free and Easy: A Spontaneous Vajra Song by Venerable Lama Gendun Rinpoche.

Free and Easy: A Spontaneous Vajra Song
By Venerable Lama Gendun Rinpoche

Happiness cannot be found
through great effort and willpower,
but is already present, in open relaxation and letting go.

Don't strain yourself,
there is nothing to do or undo.
Whatever momentarily arises in the body-mind
has no real importance at all,
has little reality whatsoever.
Why identify with, and become attached to it,
passing judgment upon it and ourselves?

Far better to simply
let the entire game happen on its own,
springing up and falling back like waves
without changing or manipulating anything
and notice how everything vanishes and
reappears, magically, again and again,
time without end.

Only our searching for happiness
prevents us from seeing it.
It's like a vivid rainbow which you pursue without ever catching,
or a dog chasing its own tail.

Although peace and happiness do not exist
as an actual thing or place,
it is always available
and accompanies you every instant.

Don't believe in the reality
of good and bad experiences;
they are like today's ephemeral weather,
like rainbows in the sky.

Wanting to grasp the ungraspable,
you exhaust yourself in vain.
As soon as you open and relax this tight fist of grasping,
infinite space is there—open, inviting and comfortable.

Make use of this spaciousness, this freedom and natural ease.
Don't search any further.

Don't go into the tangled jungle
looking for the great awakened elephant,
who is already resting quietly at home
in front of your own hearth.

Nothing to do or undo,
nothing to force,
nothing to want,
and nothing missing—

Emaho! Marvelous!
Everything happens by itself.

So there it was, a profound and beautiful Dharma song that I didn't really hear. And it was only in my rediscovery of the riches and power of our Bright Dawn lineage teachers and teachings that I felt this freedom and natural ease. One of the books I have been rereading is the essay collection by Dr. Alfred Bloom Sensei, *Living in Amida's Universal Vow*.

Reading that I kept coming back to the first essay by the great reformer in our Bright Dawn Center lineage, Kiyozawa Manshi, "The Great Path of Absolute Other Power and My Faith." In this essay he talks about his quest to find "the meaning of life at all costs." It is this quest that brought him to his belief in the Tathagata.

He describes something I believe many of us can relate to, because we have struggled with the same thing. I know I certainly can. He talks about the journey he took to his faith and his belief that self-power is absolutely useless. He said it had been a trying process and he could only reach that conclusion of the uselessness of self-power when he exhausted the entire resources of his knowledge and devices.

He would reach conclusion after conclusion of what the meaning was, then each one would be invariably undermined. As he wrote: "One can never escape this calamity so long as one is hopeful of establishing religious faith by way of logic or learning."

My recent Bright Dawn immersion experience has brought me, too, to that place Manshi Sensei hinted at; the place where all your previous conclusions about the meaning of life are undermined. They are undermined because they were formed based on logic or learning alone.

I can't tell you how many times during my life as a spiritual seeker, I have reached that place where I look back and laugh—out of frustration—laugh because I see I have been traveling for miles and miles, months and months, and sometimes years and years, heading in the wrong direction.

Now what? Now what do I have to learn to get myself oriented and walking in the right direction toward Enlightenment or whatever it is I'm seeking?

Each time I reach that place, I come closer and closer to the discovery that it's not what I have to learn or acquire, but what I must unlearn and give up.

But to be a student, one must learn, right? And there is the rub. That is the treacherous territory of being a student of Buddhism or any true spirituality or religion, and the heightened danger of being a teacher on the same path.

It was Shinran who realized in his own life that the path is not so much about Enlightenment or being reborn in the Pure Land, but about the awakening of faith and a naturalness, or "Amida's Sincerity." This awakening of faith is described by Kaneko Daiei, a student of Manshi Sensei, in his essay, "The Meaning of Salvation in the Doctrine of Pure Land Buddhism" also in the book *Living in Amida's Universal Vow.*

He describes it as "breaking through at the root of delusion." When that happens, he writes, we are broken, our self-complacency and our faith in self power, logic, and concepts is shaken. He says "we are emptied through and through" yet "at the same moment we find ourselves taken in by Amida's Sincerity" and "for the first time attain true restfulness, because our deepest root of our existential anxiety or suffering, namely ignorance, is cut through forever."

Of course this doesn't mean that we won't experience suffering as long as we remain in the world, but he says "they no longer disturb the fundamental restfulness and serenity."

All this circles back to what Rev. Gyomay Kubose teaches in so many of his essays in *Everyday Suchness* and *The Center Within*. Reread for yourself the essays "Naturalness", "Living Life", "Life without Regret", "Buddhism is Everyday Life", "Simplicity". "The Natural Way", "Gateless Gate", and "Transcending Means and Ends", to name a few.

Yes, I have been a student of these teachings … constantly whispering in my ear … while I was still trying to be a student, trying to be a teacher, hunting that illusive "self" or lack of self I thought I needed to find, and trying to go wherever I thought I needed to go to find it.

I was listening, but I wasn't hearing. I wasn't actually living my life. I was doing what I thought I should to reach the goal of … of … what? Hunting the great awakened elephant!

Running away from myself, looking beyond my own life to find it. I hadn't emptied myself through and through. No, instead, I had been loading myself up with elephant-hunting gear and elephant-hunting instructions and books. I was collecting that gear from every teacher and it was weighing me down until I was lost and spinning, not knowing what direction I was heading.

Had I listened deeply—not mouthing the words to be a model student or give the right teachings—but listened *in* me, *for* me, I would have heard. I would have heard that Enlightenment is everyday … that acceptance is transcendence

… that ends = means. And that only in emptying myself, releasing me from the tight grasp of me, that I can truly live as me.

Had I truly listened, I would have heard Rev. Gyomay Kubose saying to me "Only when one lives his life does he know its meaning." I would have heard him say, "Whatever the true inner heart says is the right way. Listen to its voice." I would have heard him say the true way "is simply the natural way." I would have heard him say that "the true self is selflessness" … the teaching of "forget yourself."

And I would have heard the voice of Rev. Akegarasu, as Shuichi Maida wrote in *Heard By Me.* He wrote, "Rev. Akegarasu is always whispering in my ear, 'There is nothing to worry about. You had better do whatever you want to do.' This is the Buddha-Dharma I heard from him."

_/|_ A deep Gassho to our precious teachers.

THE SIGN
Ken Muyo Swanson

On Monday, I had to pay a visit to the Courthouse at our local County Clerk's Office. My first Army pension payment upon reaching 60 was wrong – an annuity payment was being withheld every month for my first (ex) wife.

My divorce was over 10 years ago—I've been remarried for seven years. I thought every piece of paper the Army needed—the copies of the divorce decree and judge's and court filings, the new marriage certificate and papers, were submitted years ago. Now, I was told the holdup was because the Army wasn't sure whether the copies of the divorce decree were legal or not. They weren't "certified." Whatever that means.

So, down to the Courthouse I went…. The Clerk of Courts directed me to the files, and I was told to go through the originals concerning my divorce and to pull out the papers that I needed, and he would make copies and certify them. So, I took this long walk down memory lane, flipping through all the papers, some of which I had never seen before, It was really depressing having to relive those painful times that I thought were over, done and settled long ago.

I took the appropriate papers up to him, and I saw the following sign hanging on the wall behind the desk:

EVERYTHING IN THE PRESENT IS AN EFFECT

RESULTING FROM CAUSES IN THE PAST

WHOA! Shades of the Twelve Linked Chains of Dependent Origination! I said to him "that's a neat sign." He responded, "it's been here as long as I've been here—30 years." I asked if he was Buddhist—he said, "No, I'm Baptist." He said that most people never seemed to even notice the sign, and no one ever asked about it. I thanked him for his help and went on my way. I was thinking about my past life, who I had wanted to be, what I had wanted to do, where I had wanted to go, who I had wanted to be with, the choices I made, good and not so good, and my many failures and some success.

So, I was thinking about this karma thing—how do I make amends for those past wrongs and destructive actions and harm that were present in my life all those years ago? I realize that it was not just MY actions that I was having to deal with, but I also realize that the only person I could ever control, then and now, is myself. I feel like I wasted almost 30 years.

I recite the Noble Truths in my mind and read my books for understanding: Right Understanding, Right Thought, Right Speech, Right Action, Right Livelihood, Right Effort, Right Mindfulness, Right Concentration. I can't "Right" the past; all I can do is try to learn from it and demonstrate compassion and wisdom in my present and future life, and try to view my past with the same compassion and wisdom. Wisdom and compassion are inseparable.

Here's something I read from a 15th Century eccentric Japanese Zen Buddhist priest and poet named Ikkyu, who was also one of the creators of the formal Japanese tea ceremony:

> *Under the trees, among the rocks, a thatched hut:*
> *Verses and sacred commentaries live there together.*
> *I'll burn the book I carry in my bag,*
> *But how can I forget the verses written in my gut.*

All week long, I've had stomach problems—heartburn and acid reflux. I'm taking the usual Pepcid and Prilosec. Maybe it's all those verses written in my gut. I have to feel them churning down there for a while. Maybe I can eventually digest them, I don't know for sure. It may be with me for some time, or gone tomorrow.

I can read all the books and hear all the stories and teachings, but I know that sometimes you just really need to sit and let things settle. It's good to "understand." But you also have to experience it at the "gut" level -- for as long as it takes. Compassion and wisdom. What goes around, comes around. That is where I am today in my practice.

Another poem from Ikkyu:

> *Memories*
> *Flee and*
> *Are no more.*
> *All are empty dreams*
> *Devoid of meaning.*
>
> *Violate the reality of things*
> *And babble about*
> *"God" and "the Buddha"*
> *And you will never find*
> *The true Way.*

Palms together, and three bows to the Buddha.

BASEBALL, BUDDHISM, AND LIFE
Wendy Shinyo Haylett

I love baseball. When April comes and the season starts, it's just another reason I rejoice in the return of spring. Of course, I love the new green, the warming temperatures, the daffodils, and the bulging buds of new leaves on the trees, but the return of baseball makes everything even MORE exciting. As Al Gallagher, a baseball player in the 1970's, said, "There are three things in life which I really love: God, my family, and baseball. The only problem—once baseball season starts, I change the order around a bit."

Now, baseball doesn't possess me like some people, but I watch or listen to a game almost every day during the season . . . and sometimes two games a day. I rarely miss a Cleveland Indians game. Being a Cleveland fan, as anyone who follows baseball already knows, gives the season a little extra edge, a lot more drama, and invariably a lot of disappointment.

But for me, watching baseball is meditative. When you're watching a baseball game there's a lot of time to reflect. The season itself is long, from April to October, and the games can be verrrrrrry long. In a good pitchers' duel there can be a long time between an offensive play and the roar of the crowd. You can fall asleep watching a game in the 4th inning and wake up in the 8th without missing a hit or a score. Baseball gives you a lot of time to reflect and, well, just loaf, which most of us don't do nearly enough of.

Bill Veeck, a former Cleveland Indians' owner and the one credited for integrating the American League when he signed Larry Doby in 1947, said of baseball that it "is a game to be savored, not gulped." Like life, it's so much better when you're not thinking about getting somewhere or achieving something, but letting life itself lead you, responding to things as they are, not as you planned them or would like them to be.

One of the most important lessons baseball teaches is the spirituality of imperfection. In the book by that name, *The Spirituality of Imperfection: Storytelling and the Search for Meaning,* by Ernest Kurtz and Katherine Ketcham, the authors, write "baseball, alone in sport, considers errors to be part of the game, part of its rigorous truth." In baseball, errors are tallied and publicized and flashed on the screen for every team and every player. Errors are accepted as part of the game.

Baseball expects mistakes from its players. And, its most coveted accomplishment, the so-called "perfect game" can only be achieved if the pitcher is perfect AND his teammates also play perfectly, with no errors.

Jodo and Shin Buddhism teaches us that we are bombu. It is our nature to make mistakes. We are NOT perfect players. We make errors. But it's OK. That is who we are. And, as David Brazier Sensei says, I'm not OK and you're not OK, and that is perfectly OK! Thankfully, though, our errors aren't counted and published in the morning news every day.

But there's more to baseball that models the Dharma very closely. I'll use the three marks of existence, as the three bases, that as Buddhists, we try to come to an understanding and acceptance of: Impermanence, unsatisfactoriness, and lack of a discrete self or an "I." These three marks characterize the interconnectedness / interdependence, impermanence, and change that we accept in the Dharma.

First base is lack of a discrete self. As a team sport, baseball is not just about the pitcher. Even when the pitcher is throwing strikes, if the ball gets away from the catcher, or the centerfielder can't find the ball in the sun, there will be an error and the hitter will get a base or two.

The interdependence of baseball is awesome and it sometimes seems nearly impossible that all the players, and contributing causes and conditions can come together positively to score runs and have a dominating offensive win or to rule defensively in a no-hitter or one-hitter.

No matter how much we try and wish to, it is unlikely that we can become a Buddha by ourselves alone. In fact, in truth, we cannot do much of anything by ourselves alone. Self power only gets us so far. Other power is needed to round the bases and slide into home safely.

Second base is unsatisfactoriness. Baseball can break your heart and in a long season, lasting from Spring to Fall, with more than 160 regular season games, players and fans alike can go through many, many ups and downs, 11th inning walk-off home runs for a victory, and crazy-making, gut-wrenching losses.

As a Cleveland fan, I can testify that every spring when the Indians charge to the lead in the Central Division, I'm dreaming of exciting post-season games, and a World Series maybe. Then they hit a period where they lose 8 games in a row and I see this year is going to be just like last year, and I get disappointed and don't want to watch another game.

But I do. I have hope. I keep going.

And then there are those games that you are sure your team is going to win . . . going into the ninth inning, up 4 runs . . . and then the opposing team takes the game from you with a last inning, seven-run hitting display.

But as Tommy Lasorda said, "No matter how good you are, you're going to lose one-third of your games. No matter how bad you are, you're going to win one-third of your games. It's the other third that makes the difference."

Life is like that. Some days you think that this day just couldn't get any better and maybe, just maybe, you're in for a great week . . . or month . . . or year. But, just as quickly, in the next few days, something happens to remind you that life is not perfect and you just have to keep playing anyway. There will be days where everything will flow and days where nothing works. But we keep playing through the season.

Third base is impermanence. Like a good pitcher, life is constantly changing. It throws you curveballs, sinkers, change-ups, sliders, fastballs. But we have one job to do: to keep hitting until the right pitch comes. We keep fouling them off until we can get a hit. We keep trying and, if we get a hit, we have to commit to run the bases. If we strike out, we have another chance at bat.

In the long season of baseball and life, we have to prepare to play through a lot of different weather. Snow at the beginning and end of the season, rain delays and rain-outs, blinding sun where outfielders lose the ball, and 100+ degree temperatures draining your energy. Weather disrupts our plans, brings trees down on our cars and houses, flood our houses, and can take our lives. We keep playing through the changes nature throws at us.

And sometimes you get traded and you're no longer a Cleveland Indian, but a designated hitter for the New York Yankees. And in life, we rarely stay in the same job, with the same company, or live in the same house, the same city, or even the same state or country. We make the best of it, though, and even thrive in the change.

Sometimes we're on deck, expectant to hit against the pitcher we've had great success against, and the opposing team's coach replaces that pitcher for a lefty-lefty match up ... and our current record against left-handed pitchers is abysmal.

Sometimes we steal base and get caught, retiring the side with three outs. And sometimes we get away with it. In our lives, we have all done or said things we shouldn't have, or aren't proud of. Sometimes others are aware and call us on them, sometimes only we know what we've done. And sometimes we are punished by a system: our parents or the legal system.

Yet, caught, punished, or not, we have faith in the transcendent order of life. Of karmic action. Whatever we do, we know that our actions cause other actions and we must be prepared to face the consequences of those actions.

The sports writer, Paul Gallico, wrote that "no other game in the world is as tidy and dramatically neat as baseball, with cause and effect, crime and punishment . . ." And back to Bill Veeck again, he says that baseball is an "orderly thing in a very unorderly world. If you get three strikes, even the best lawyer in the world can't get you off."

We've covered three, so now home plate. And home plate is this: no matter what life throws at us, the best we can do is, as we "Bright Dawners" say, to "keep going."

I grew up with three brothers and a father who loved baseball. I suspect it is what incited my love of the game. It stirs a deep emotional response of safety, comfort, contentment, and summer. The low-grade hum of baseball crowds on the radio or TV, the rhythm of the play-by-play and color announcers, punctuated by whistles and cheers, is like crickets on a warm summer night, the soothing sound of a gentle rain, or the hum of a Buddhist chant.

And while fingering my 108-bead mala, I think of what I just learned about the baseball itself—that there are 108 stitches on a baseball—did anyone know that!?

I'll close by echoing the words of the poet Sharon Olds when she says, "Baseball is reassuring. It makes me feel as if the world is not going to blow up."

Sometimes we take ourselves too seriously . . . and we take our spirituality too seriously. Sometimes the only way to invite our soul is to loaf, observe a blade of grass, or to play ball!

So today, go through your day remembering to be happy. Reach out. Share. Smile. Hug. Make each day a holiday and celebrate just living.

LUCY
Kenneth Muyo Swanson

I was working on a report for my Lay Ministry class... then Lucy (our dog) died. On Thursday, it was pretty clear she was fading. It'd been eight weeks since she stopped eating and about a week since she refused water. I washed her face, cleaned her eyes, sat and talked with her -- telling her that it was ok for her to leave and that she could come back and raise another family like ours. I read to her about Jizos. She had a clean bed and blanket, she was comfortable. I went to work. Jennifer comes home about an hour later -- she called me a few hours later -- about 6:30 pm, Lucy stiffened out her legs and sighed. She passed comfortably. Jennifer washed her, got a clean sheet and put her in her bed in a cool place by the door. When I came home from work at 1 a.m., we took her to the Animal Emergency Center. Lucy could still teach vet nurses and technicians there, so we thought that was good. Then she would be cremated. We went home pretty exhausted but felt that Lucy was in good, caring hands.

I had gotten a little flack during the past few weeks about "Isn't it inhumane to not put down your dog -- isn't she suffering? -- she's going on 17 years old, she's just a dog," etc. No, she was not suffering. No, she was not "just a dog." She was family -- she was there when Johanna came home from school, she was there when anyone was sick, she protected us, she was our alarm clock in the morning. She never woke up grouchy, and she never went to bed mad. Animals are pretty incredible.

Lucy knew that this was an impermanent world and that every flavor, every smell was shared-- it was a communal experience. She seemed to know what "oneness" is -- she really did have Buddha-nature. We learned a lot from her. Two weeks ago, she slid down off the couch to the floor where she poured over the latest Oneness from Bright Dawn (I assure you this was NOT staged!).

It was a good lesson for us in how things happen in their own time. I think back to how my baby sister, born with a heart defect and sent home from the hospital to die, was kept in the bedroom -- it was months before she passed. I don't remember anything about it now. It was good to have Lucy at home during her final months, comfortable, cared for. It was stressful, sad, sometimes messy, sometimes funny, but that is all part of the cycle of living and dying.

I found a Gatha for a Memorial Gathering that seemed right:

> We do not die—we cannot die;
> We only change our state in life
> When these earth temples fall and lie
> Unmoving 'mid the world's wide strife.

There is no death in this wide world;
But one eternal scene of change;
The flag of life is never furled,
It only taketh wider range.

By ourselves is evil done,
By ourselves we pain endure,
By ourselves we cease from wrong,
By ourselves become we pure.

No one saves us but ourselves,
No one can, and no one may;
We ourselves must walk the path,
Buddhas merely teach the way.

Who so is compassionate is everywhere beloved; by the kind and good Lucy
was prized as a friend, and at death her heart is full of peace.
May It Be So

THE SILENT PIANO
David Nichiyo Abatangelo

The other day my seven year old son, Conal, asked me to come and look at something in the dining room. "Watch this," he said, standing at the piano with a big smile. He proceeded to press five keys, one at a time, all the way down without making a sound.

"That's great!" I said, but little did Conal appreciate how much he had really impressed me.

I took piano lessons for almost ten years when I was younger--then went about 25 years without a piano. A few years ago, I started taking lessons again. When I did, I had the goal of really mastering a couple of showstoppers.

The vision in my head:

> *My wife and I are invited to my boss' house for cocktails. I notice the piano. I walk over and nonchalantly pluck a couple of keys.*
>
> *"Oh, do you play?" my boss asks.*
>
> *"A little." I say coyly. And then I sit down and rip through Chopin's "Revolutionary Etude"--a flurry of arpeggios and crescendos that flies through hundreds of notes in two minutes and eight seconds. I calmly pick up my martini and rejoin the party as the conversation restarts. Having duly impressed my boss, the Halo Effect carries over into the office and I am quickly promoted.*

So, with this in mind, I work on the "Revolutionary Etude." At some point in the lesson my teacher inevitably says, "Hmmph," and I never finish the piece. I play the first page quite impressively but find I don't have the patience to slow down enough to really work through the whole thing.

Soon thereafter, my teacher begins the lesson with "Anyone fool can play loud and fast. It takes talent to play slowly and softly." For the next half year we play slowly. Sl-o-o-o-o-o-wly. We talk about Glenn Gould and play a lot of Bach. Bach did not put time signatures on his music and Gould gained international renown for his interpretations of Bach--which he of course played much more slowly than anyone else.

After six months, I could play slowly.

And guess what? It is much more difficult to play slowly than quickly. Mechanically, it might be more difficult to move your fingers quickly but it takes a great deal of emotional and mental discipline to slow down and maintain a tempo throughout a piece.

For the last five months or so, we started every lesson with some exercises designed to build finger strength and independence of hands (i.e. be able to play very softly with one hand and loudly with the other). It involves doing exactly what Conal did-striking the key without creating a sound. Trust me-it is very, very difficult to do. At least I find it very, very difficult--especially on a poorly regulated piano.

Typically, every couple of months, my piano teacher gives me a couple of books to take home. I find a song or two that I really enjoy and play it throughout the week--looking forward to playing it at my next lesson. We go through our exercises and then I play the song. Inevitably, I play four or five measures and he stops me to go back over something--to play it more slowly, carefully, or tenderly.

So, after having spent half a year playing songs as slowly and steadily as possible, and the last five months playing them as softly as possible, I took a new book home a couple of weeks ago and found a piece I really liked--Chopin's "Nocturne in E minor". Surprisingly, when I played it at my lesson my teacher didn't stop me even once. "That," he said, "was beautiful."

I told him that I thought that I had sped up a little in a couple of parts. He told me that I had but maybe by about two percent.

"Wow," I thought. I had played it slowly, softly and beautifully. But I had not just played it slowly and softly, I had played with an emotion that I couldn't have mustered three years or even five months ago. Not only had I played better, I was more fully aware of what I had played, sensing even that slight unintended increase in tempo. And, I had done it almost effortlessly and subconsciously.

My other son has special educational needs and we have had incredible difficulties with the local school district to fully execute his independent education plan. After trying and trying to work collaboratively with the school we've finally given up and had to engage a lawyer. I can't remember anything that has gotten me as angry. When we met with the lawyer he said that he was going to bring an intern to take notes because he gets so agitated at these meetings that he forgets to take them himself. He said that he would be the bad guy so that my wife and I would seem reasonable by comparison. To be honest, at that point, I didn't care whether the school administration thought I was reasonable--I just wanted to walk into that room and lay into him and every one of his administrators.

But, that would be the easy thing to do--any fool can play loud and fast. This is true with emotions. It is easy to get angry, rehearse the pithy zingers then let fly. It's much harder to look with compassion at those who are failing my son. I've spent a lot of time meditating and contemplating in the CTA zendo (i.e. the 136 Express bus) on the way to work. It has been hard to let go of my rage and view the people involved in my son's education without emotion, and even harder to view them with compassion. I've focused on slowing down my emotions and thinking compassionate thoughts. And as I do this, I am more aware when I do start to get angry and better able to pull back.

But, this is what we must do in our practice. We must work hard at playing slowly and softly. And, we must do it in an unregulated life. Just like few pianists have the benefit of playing on a perfectly regulated piano where each key has the same feel and response as the key next to it, few people have a similarly regulated life. Life is out of tune, keys stick. There are so many variables outside our control that even the best laid plans can go awry. Perhaps this is why it is so important to find time for meditation and retreat.

As we focus on developing our compassion and awareness of our true feelings we are better able to control our anger, greed and delusion. Anger is always an affliction.

It was interesting that Conal had been able to strike the keys without making a noise. Although he had obviously worked at it a little before showing me, it did not take him a lot of effort. He just pressed the keys and never thought about whether the piano was in tune or not.

Bright Dawn Dharma Glimpses:

LAY MINISTER CLASS #3

DANDELIONS
Michael Shinyo Lawrence

Today I noticed dandelions popping up everywhere. I began thinking back to when I was a little boy. Dandelions were beautiful flowers, not weeds! I would pick them and give them to my mother, who would then fill a glass of water to put them in as if they were special flowers. There were a lot of fun things to do with dandelions. We would string them together and wear them around our necks, on our heads, or around our arms. We also would use them to mark ourselves up or mark others with them. It was even more fun when they turned to seeds. Then we could pick them and blow the seeds everywhere. Adults did not see this as fun at all. Blowing seeds everywhere just meant we were planting more weeds. Dandelions are hard to control and they spread so fast. Seeing all the bright and sunny dandelions today made me think about what it means to see things through a child's eyes. Children can see things with wonderment. It's nice to remember what that is like. It's nice to see the beauty in what may be perceived as ugly or weeds. Maybe dandelions can symbolize the Dharma and as we blow the seeds everywhere, the Dharma can spread and grow.

SHARED SPIRIT
Jeff Wayo Ward

As is often the case when my friends and I gather, the conversation turns from role playing games, comic books. and other nerd related stuff to headier topics like politics, history, and of course religion. Being the only centrist liberal, Irish/native American Buddhist on the "panel" I'm usually the one coming out of left field. But the other day a very conservative Methodist buddy of mine stated "besides all the technical stuff, Buddhism and Christianity are teaching the same thing." Another buddy replied "the better Christian I become the more Buddhist I feel."

I thought, "Wow, here's an intriguing notion." I mean obviously the two are not the same; being raised a strict southern Baptist, I really am uncomfortable with the Dogma as it was presented to me. But still there can be some unity. I think Buddha would have accepted "turn the other cheek" and Christ would have accepted the idea of Right Livelihood. How fortunate that communication between East and West is so easy today. While not sacrificing our own beliefs, we should reach out on those points of similarity, accept what we share, and work together to better improve the human condition. Instead of dividing the world into us and them, or more importantly us versus them, we should just be people compassionately embracing one another. Yes, our faith is defined by the 'technical stuff' but the spirit of faith is our fuel and that spirit is shared by many.

GRATEFUL TO THE LAST!
Shaku Sayo Shenphen

"Gratitude IS the spiritual life." These are the words of my teacher. Words I try to live by every day. No matter what the day brings, gratitude is important to foster.

It is said that the more we're grateful, the more we attract more things to be grateful for.

Gratitude is said to be the remedy to guard against greed. Being thankful helps us lessen our attachment to wanting more. We are satisfied just as things are with nothing lacking.

Living in gratitude is a practice. The practice of being free from attachment to desires or wanting more. To flowing freely without pretense or artificiality. To know nothing is lacking. Of course we will always need things to survive, but gratitude is key to never needing more and more.

If we can live a life of gratitude, a life filled with a thankful heart, when we meet the end of our physical, karmic existence, we can leave this life with nothing but a thankful mind. A mind that rests in a calm abiding state of peace. Our last thought is simply thank you.

I AM THE GREATEST MAN IN THE WORLD!!
Toyo T. Katamori

How can it be said? Can I or others think of such a title for me? Sure, why not? It has been said. I am the greatest man in the world. As well as being said, I myself think that I am the greatest man in the world. Why such a title? Why not? I am a good man, a hell of a friend, a fellow among fellows and even a fraternal brother of good report and well recommended. I am the greatest man in the world, and that sums it up to just that. Is this thinking too highly of oneself? Not at all. Why wouldn't you? You, that man in the skin on the bones your head is attached to, think that way. You! And only you. If any one person in this world is going to think of you as the greatest man in the world, let it be you, and firstly starting with you. It begins now, not yesterday, and not tomorrow, but only now with you.

Sure, yesterday you were the greatest man in the world, and today certainly you are the greatest man in the world, and no doubt tomorrow you will hold that title true. It is true and only truth holds witness to that title. Authentic truth is all it takes. Everything has a beginning or is a continuation of a process of life. Being the greatest man in the world is in there revolving, around and around and around. It may have simply started like the big bang theory. BOOM!! There it is, you are the greatest man in the world. Can this title be compared to? No! every one man is his own separate greatest man in the world. Was this done by only you? Absolutely no way. Interdependency was and is the only way this title can ever be bestowed upon that skin on those bones that support that head.

Every action has a reaction, and every action is causation with its effects being the perquisites to being the greatest man in the world. These actions are whatever they may be, and no one action is ever greater than the other. What the effects of that action have left to someone is the prerequisite to this title. Building the tallest building in the world is the same as replacing the batteries in the Wii game controller for your daughter so she can continue to play her favorite horse game. Holding up a door so your friend can shore it up, level it, and secure it grandly is the same as a man setting foot onto the moon. Interdependency is a grand part in all the greatest men in the world. Every action you have taken and will take is dependent upon your present self, and what your self generally feels it to be must be considered. Ourselves are reliant upon those around us and every one around us is dependent on our actions. Walk tall, look up, carry on and continue to be the greatest man in the world. The world is dependent upon that!

WHAT'S IN YOUR SOUP?
Niko Byoyo Burkhardt

There are always so many topics to choose from when it comes to writing a Dharma Glimpse and sometimes I don't even know what it will be when I sit down and start typing. What is most relevant to my experience right now is usually what I choose to write about and typically there are others who can relate to that. One of my many treasured mentors and teachers is an extraordinary woman by the name of Stephanie Mines. Dr. Mines has an extensive background in psychology with a specialty in the resolution of shock and trauma. At some point in her very successful career, she realized that in order to truly and completely resolve the effects of trauma in the nervous system, one must be able to re pattern the neural pathways that were formed as a result of this trauma. The brain's ability to do this is called neural plasticity. What Dr. Mines discovered is that a patient could talk about their trauma all day long and have an intellectual understanding of it, but it takes more than intellect to process it fully. One of the fastest ways to re pattern neurology is through the physical body, specifically, therapeutic touch. As a licensed psychologist, Dr. Mines was forbidden to touch her patient in the therapy process.

"My studies of Jin Shin began long before I got my doctorate in psychology. I had a Jin Shin practice before I went back to school for my doctorate. Once I was a psychologist there were rules about combining touch with psychotherapy so I maintained two separate practices for a long time. Finally I realized how arbitrary and strange it was to support this unnatural division. Ultimately I closed my practice completely so that I could represent a new paradigm of treatment for the holistic and thorough resolution of shock and trauma. My system, the TARA Approach, treats the whole person and does not maintain the artificial and inaccurate separation of mind and body." - -Dr. Mines

Thus was born, the **TARA** Approach or also called, Jin Shin Tara. **TARA** stands for two things; it is an acronym for Tools for Awakening Resources and Awareness, and it is named after the Tibetan Buddha Green Tara. Dr. Mines studies with a Tibetan teacher in Colorado, but does not claim affiliation with any particular religion.

You might be wondering what this all has to do with soup! When I was training with Dr. Mines, she talked about the neurochemical "soup" that a fetus is basting in when in the mother's womb. This soup is determined by the mother's physical, mental and emotional health as well as her environment. Factors that can impact the nutritional value of this soup are positive and negative. For instance, if the mother is experiencing a great deal of stress during pregnancy, her body will produce many toxins and stress hormones that can be detrimental to the development of the baby. On the other hand, if the mother is joyful and at peace, the baby will benefit from this greatly. When we are a developing fetus, we have no choice about our home and what kind of soup we are marinating in. This soup will determine a lot about our physical health and predispose us to behavioral patterns for the rest of our lives. Every human on this planet has been influenced by this process which can seem to some as irreversible damage. For those who have access to the skills and resources, there is hope for change through neural plasticity! The good news is you can make your own soup!

What I have learned is this: I am an adult and can make my own choices and I can choose the ingredients for my soup that will benefit not only me but anyone who wants to share it with me. I have a lot of good resources now to choose from. Jin Shin Tara is the staple stock for my soup and to bulk it up, I add the eightfold path and the four noble truths. The combination of these ingredients creates a highly nutritional and delicious food source to nurture my body, mind and spirit. It gives me the strength and awareness to pull up destructive behavioral patterns by the roots. It empowers me to know that I belong on this planet and I deserve to experience the nourishment of the universe.

I recall a quote from the Buddha that goes something like this, "If a man were to offer you a plate of spoiled food, would you accept it?"

Everyday the people around us will offer us the chance to share their soup. It is up to us to determine if their soup has the ingredients that will nourish us or harm us. Sometimes, we feel obligated to share toxicity with friends and family because we fear that if we refuse, we will offend them. For example, the urge to participate in family gossip can be alluring, especially if there is a neural pathway for this behavior around certain family members. While it can seem harmless, it may impede our spiritual growth and enable the negative behavior. Many people have family systems that depend on each member to contribute negativity or toxicity in order to operate.

The only way the family has ever related to each other is through this pattern. For example, your family gets together for holidays and the traditional food everyone brings is mostly fatty, fried foods and sweet desserts. You have recently been changing your lifestyle and eating habits to support a healthier existence. You have eliminated fried foods and refined sugar from your diet and are feeling better than you ever have. You anticipate that when you go to this gathering, not only will there not be any food for you to eat but your family may give you a hard time about being different from them. They feel threatened by your individuation from the family system. For a moment, you consider making up an excuse and not attending the gathering because it may cause you to give in and eat the unhealthy food. Instead, you take a container of your own soup to a family picnic so you don't have to eat the unhealthy buffet that is laid out! That way you can spend time with your family and protect your own well-being. This formula can be used anytime in any situation as a way to move through a toxic world without becoming sick.

FRUIT OF MEDITATION
Jeff Wayo Ward

I got ready for meditation. As always I prepared my spot by lighting incense and candles. I'm sure we are all familiar with the phenomenon of a light source "burning" an image on the back of our eyes as we close them. We get the silhouette of the last image we saw. For me as I sat there on my zafu, that image was a statue of Shakyamuni Buddha that I have as the centerpiece of my altar. The black silhouette of the Buddha was surrounded by the glow of the candles, burning beyond my closed eyelids, which appeared in the shape of a pair of hands in Gassho on my retina. The image of the Buddha seemed to reach out and the black of his silhouette extinguished the red glow and my inner vision went completely black. No image remained burned on my retina.

In religions as a whole we often attribute the deity, prophet etc, as a guiding light. But this image made me see it in a different way. The Buddha and his Law can be seen as a gentile shade comforting and protecting us from the harsh burning light of our illusions. Just as we take refuge under the shade of a tree on a hot sunny day, we take refuge in the Buddha. His law comforts us, and lessens the burning of our ego-fueled selves, so that our True self can enjoy the gentle ephemeral breeze of universal oneness.

Now I'm not implying that this was in any way a mystical event. It was mere physics and biology acting accordingly to nature, but that such an image resulted from natural processes and the circumstances of the moment serves to remind us the Dharma is present everywhere,; we just have to open our eyes to see it.

CHALICE
Morris Sekiyo Sullivan

I give a lot of talks at Unitarian Universalist churches, and almost all of the churches start their services by lighting a chalice on the altar. The chalice is the symbol of Unitarian Universalism, and it occurred to me one morning while I was speaking at a Vietnamese Buddhist monastery that the chalice is a pretty good metaphor for Buddhist practice, too.

A chalice typically consists of a round-bottomed cup or goblet-like container which is attached to a sturdy base. Both of those elements are necessary. If you just had the cup, you could pour water into it, but you'd just end up with a mess—the cup would fall over and it would just go everywhere. In order for the cup to hold its contents, you have to have the base. So without that foundation, the cup is useless.

Obviously, the base wouldn't be worth much by itself, either. You might have a very decorative base, but on its own you still have nothing that will hold your water.

There's another component, too. This one might be a little less obvious, but very important—it's the space inside the cup. The cup itself is just the container for the space, really. Without the space, there's no place for the liquid to go.

Our chalice of spiritual practice has these same elements—a base, which is made up of knowledge and understanding, and a cup, made from practice. And that creates a sturdy container to fill with wisdom.

Without a basic understanding of the main teachings, then meditating, chanting, making offerings, even taking the precepts don't really have all that much meaning. You don't have to know everything, but you have to know enough to give your spiritual practice a firm foundation.

On the other hand, we can get really caught up in learning about Buddhism—learning scriptures, memorizing lineages, learning Japanese or Pali or Sanskrit terminology, and so on, but never get around to practicing.

But knowledge, by itself, is not the dharma. To know about a thing is not the same as knowing the thing. There's the Zen saying: "the finger pointing to the moon is not the moon." If we're not trying to live this knowledge and understanding, we can't experience the dharma for ourselves.

Once you have the foundation of knowledge and the cup of practice, there is a space in which wisdom can settle. I like to call that space "faith." In Buddhism, faith arises out of that foundation of understanding and is shaped by practice. Faith becomes the open space into which wisdom can flow.

Sometimes we might find that we know a lot and practice a lot, but our hearts are still full of preconceptions and prejudices. If our space is already full, we need to let go of these things to make room for wisdom to flow into that space we created with our knowledge and practice.

As you do this, by the way, you will find room for more and more wisdom. This chalice we're building is kind of magical: the more wisdom we have, the bigger our foundation of knowledge grows, and the more refined our practice becomes, so our reservoir of wisdom gets larger and larger.

JEFF'S SON
Jeff Wayo Ward

This Dharma Glimpse comes courtesy of my three-year-old son. It was a warm day, so we were playing outside on his big wooden swing-set. We were sitting on the deck portion for the slide. I lifted my hand and began to point out the limbs of the trees above us, then the clouds in all their funny shapes and wisps, and the BIG blue sky. As I was showing him all this, reinforcing words to their image and definition, everything we are told to do to ensure good communication development, he placed his hands together at chest level and said "Do Gassho Daddy" (although when he says it, it sounds somewhat like *queso*). He sometimes kneels beside me and participates in my harmony and gratitude Gassho. At the moment, he didn't understand the profoundness of the coincidence of his statement, but I was moved by it.

Children are so removed from the dullness of everyday life. He does have his own set of attachments, of course, to certain foods and toys. Sharing is a work in progress at this age. Still, he isn't caught up in self-image and motivated by it. He is who he is. Even though we are still working through the occasional tantrum, he is at peace for the most part. He does have some inborn me/mine reflex, but he is free, at this age, of the illusionary concern of status and self-importance.

Obviously, children don't have to worry about jobs and bills, as we adults do, but we can learn a lesson from them. He has now entered the stage of imagination or pretend play, and does so very creatively. This is a self-reflecting moment for me; a three-year old is a very good mirror. He will pretend to feed his action figures or nurture them in some way; 'they' never fight. He tripped over a toy recently and, rather than throw it or kick it, he put it in 'timeout'.

He's like a living Dharma lesson. When observing him, I remember to let life happen and not get caught up in myself, to act with compassion, and certainly to apply the Eightfold Path. Right speech is crucial with a three-year old.

BLUE HERON
Michael Shinyo Lawrence

Blue Heron flying
leaves changing, colors falling
The sun shines at night

For me, the Blue Heron is a symbol of Buddhism, or everyday life. Watching this bird fly makes me stop. Time seems to stop with its flight. Gyomay-sensei wrote that the art of haiku is the Buddhist life expressed in poetic form. This seems very true. Haiku typically contain things from nature and seasonal references. This is my first attempt at haiku and I hope to learn more about it. The Blue Heron flying is something I think of when I need to stop and focus on here and now. I cannot describe why this is. I know if you get the chance to watch it fly, you'll understand. Leaves changing is the seasonal reference and also symbolic of impermanence. Colors falling is pertaining to not only the leaves in fall, but also how we see things. We may have our own perspectives or colors that we see our world. The sun shines at night means that even though we do not see the sun, does not mean it is not shining. It is also a reference to time. I plan to someday learn haiku as it is clearly a poetic expression of the Buddhist life.

DHARMA OF GUMP
Shaku Sayo Shenphen

I have an affinity for films. I always find a message within the story. Even the most ridiculous and mundane of films have a message. They have Dharma.

I was lying in bed once more this week due to yet another visit from the Cold Buddha. Again I enjoyed being sick and used this time to gain wisdom. So instead of just lying in bed, I decided to watch a movie. I watched one of my favorite movies, *Forrest Gump*.

This movie has always inspired me on so many levels. For me, *Forrest Gump* is a great Dharma film. Forrest himself is the perfect model of a "Seeker" without trying to be one.

He was able to simply live life. Forrest had the mind of a simple child -- in awe with all things and experiences, even running, which we tend to take for granted, was so much more to him. During the scene where he ran for close to three years, when asked if he was running for world peace he simply answered, "I just felt like running." That's it. No more reasoning needed. He just ran.

Forrest's life in the movie seems to be one coincidence after another. I personally do not believe in coincidence. If I did, my whole life would be nothing more than one coincidence after another. For Forrest opportunities presented themselves. Some would say he didn't know any better because of his mental capacity. But can we say we know any better? If we did, would we not be Buddhas? So Forrest is in the same samsaric boat as us. He simply enjoyed the trip and acted freely, like the stream. He flowed through life. Struggles and all, he lived and enjoyed many of history's greatest moments. Not because he chose to be there but because he was free and able to be simply be a part of history which too flows freely.

We see that, like our own existence, his life was filled with difficulties. As the Four Noble Truths teach us, difficulties are a natural part of life. However, Forrest was never compliant. Even when he had braces on his feet, he still tried his best to live as a normal child. Even when people put him down, he kept going. He didn't seek vengeance or sit around plotting how he was going to make others eat their own words. He was simply inspired to do better.

His mother was his greatest teacher. "Mama always said… Life is like a box of chocolates. You never know what you're gonna get." She was his Buddha.

Forrest had the Bodhisattva heart. During the scenes that took place in Vietnam during the war, he risked his life saving his platoon, even though guns were flaring, bombs erupting, and was told by his long life friend Jenny to not be a hero, but to run, he still went back into "the fire" to save his friend, Bubba, and his platoon. He did so without a second thought.

When we look at the character of Forrest Gump we are inspired. We are inspired to live the moment; to live simply without all the extra mental baggage that the ego creates.

We should strive to live like Gump. Free from concepts and over intellectualizing.

This is the Dharma of Gump.

ACKNOWLEDGING LIMITATIONS
Niko Byoyo Burkhardt

Recently, our group has been exploring the topic of realizing enlightenment through whatever means we have. As a group, humans tend toward the dramatic and glamorous, so sometimes we think we will get to enlightenment by a grand gesture or event. I have been exploring the concept of enlightenment through acknowledging limitations over the past few weeks, and find it very liberating.

There are so many judgments we have as individuals, as a society or culture, about what we "should" or "should not" be doing. For instance. someone with a very strong work ethic can feel very useless, unless they are constantly engaged in some result-oriented task. When we encounter limitations in life, whether financial, physical or mental, we tend to judge ourselves and feel guilt.

In the past few weeks, I have had a chance to choose a different response to my own limitations. Rather than feeling guilty or defeated, I have experienced acceptance. After acceptance sets in for a while, I was able to see reasons to appreciate these limitations, and have been able to use them as a springboard for new opportunities I could not have seen before. To me, this is a glimpse of enlightenment, and it keeps me going when things seem too challenging.

As long as we are in resistance to a problem, we cannot see the way out. By resisting, we are in a state of mind that believes in duality. There is a problem and then there is me: they are two separate entities. By practicing acceptance, we become one with limitation, and thereby are empowered to move past it.

THE SPIDER BODHISATTVA
Morris Sekiyo Sullivan

From *Wisdom, Compassion, Serenity: First Steps on the Buddhist Path.*

I wanted to go home.

When you tell people you're going on a 10-day meditation retreat, some will answer, "Oh, that's going to be so peaceful! You'll be so calm!" I guess they imagine blissful yogis in diaphanous robes bobbing peacefully in the ether, buoyed by the sweet tones resonating from singing bowls.

In many ways, however, training the mind is like training the body: Yes, in the end you'll feel better and you might even enjoy some of it. But it will be hard work, and there's probably going to be some pain. Prepared as I was, by sundown on Day Four of a 10-day silent Vipassana retreat near the Georgia-Florida border, I was ready to leave.

Don't misunderstand—the retreat was flawlessly organized. The food was good, and we were very well supported by the volunteers. I didn't mind the silence, and it was great to have an uninterrupted period for meditation where I could focus on the activity in my own mind.

Except for the last 10 minutes or so of the twice-daily "Sitting of Strong Determination" (Vipassana-speak for "not moving for an hour") I was enjoying my time in the meditation hall. I didn't even mind that the guy sitting behind me kept nodding off and snoring.

But I missed home. I missed my wife. I missed my dogs. There were too many arbitrary-seeming rules. The rigid sequestering of the men from the women seemed jarringly archaic. The flesh-and-blood teacher in residence wasn't very helpful, and the recorded chanting, so different from the more rhythmic Thai and Japanese styles I'd done before, crept cruelly up and down my spine like nails scraping across a chalkboard.

What really threw me, however, was the ringing in my ears. In the silence, my occasional mild tinnitus had grown into an unrelenting drone of chainsaw-wielding cicadas.

Did I mention I wanted to go home?

A road ran through the retreat center compound. It led to a short trail into the Southeast Georgia pinewoods. To ease the stiffness in my knees, I walked to the end of the trail and did a little qigong and then returned to sit next to a pond by the meditation hall.

I noticed a spider about an inch long slowly working his way up the stem of a spindly weed. I watched it reach the tip of the plant and then swing off into the breeze, riding a thin strand of silk to another weed. Strand by strand, the spider patiently constructed an intricate pattern of interlaced silk.

The bell rang, calling us to the meditation hall for the evening session. I rose and moved slowly toward the web. Putting my hands together in gassho and bowing slightly, I whispered a thank you and promised to dedicate the evening's practice to the spider.

As I did, I noticed my yearning for home ease up as my heart opened slightly. I was looking forward to the meditation and to being able to dedicate any merit I accrued to the little spider that clung to the web out by the pond.

After breakfast the next morning, I walked over to the pond. The spider was nowhere to be seen; its web hung limp under the weight of thick dewdrops. By lunchtime, no sign of it remained, but that evening, I again sat by the pond and watched the spider as it patiently, strand-by-strand, created its marvelous little mandala of sticky silk.

Each day thereafter, humidity, sun and wind would tear down the web. Each evening, the spider would rebuild it.

One morning, a cold front moved through the South. It rained most of the day; when the sky cleared, a frigid, biting wind blew across the pond. The spider didn't appear that evening. I tried to warm it in my heart as I cultivated metta during the evening practice. Apparently a night spent huddled and hungry in the weeds is just a natural part of life for a spider. It returned the next evening to patiently re-weave its web.

Like the ringing in my ears, the desire to go home early never completely disappeared, but the my resolve was strengthened by the patient determination the spider manifested as naturally and *unselfconsciously* as the breeze ripples the surface of the pond.

On the final morning, I walked to the pond. The sun had not yet risen, but I could make out the ghostly shape of the web faintly outlined with dew in the fading moonlight. The spider had gone to the weeds for refuge. I put my hands together and bowed.

LIFE IS....
Jeff Wayo Ward

The other day was a typical Tuesday: I finished work, picked the kids up from daycare and came home. As we settled in, my son went off to gather up toys and crayons and everything else he needs for his afternoon. He began to play and I sat on the couch with my daughter who is two months old now. I propped her up on my legs so we could see eye-to-eye.

I began really talking to her—not just baby sounds, but real conversation, albeit simple. She suddenly got a crooked little grin on her face, and made a cooing noise that sound quite like a giggle. It was just a brief moment, but it was really a moment of clarity for me. It was as if for those few seconds the whole Universe came into focus to me. I saw the beauty of Life.

We so much speak of suffering and attachments and the vile poisons—I think we cloud out the simple joy in drawing breath each day. Life is truly amazing if we allow it to be. The very process of the wheel of Life is miraculous. From the chemical reaction of photosynthesis to the complexity of the food chain which sustains us all, to birth itself, it can all be seen as a wonderful occurrence of Oneness.

Life is a complete cosmic organism breathing deeply with each breath we draw. As we live we give vitality to Life, we are creation and creation is us—all of us, with no separation. I encourage everyone to be the Breath and Blood of Life itself, to live authentically in this Unity of Wholeness.

I guess it was a powerful giggle, but what should one expect from a two month old. Laugh and the world laughs with you.

A TRUE GIFT
Shaku Sayo Shenphen

One Christmas morning I was gifted by presents from a dear and close friend of mine. I felt a sense of emptiness. I was grateful for them, but it felt empty. I thought to myself "Wow, my Dharma practice must really be going well. I'm not at all excited about these gifts."

Later that morning, I went to the gas station before going to visit family. As I was making my purchase, the attendant stopped to ask me what I was going to do for Christmas. I told him I was going to visit family. He asked if I was going to have a big feast and eat a lot?

"First I have to cook everything, but yes," I replied.

He continued by sharing with me how he and his family were up all night until six in the morning, cooking and preparing their feast. He was late to work because he had only gotten one hour of sleep. However, his face was lit up. He was really happy.

After he finished with my purchase he said "Merry Christmas!" I replied the same and that I hoped he enjoyed the food.

When I got back into my friend's car, I stopped for a moment. I realized that I had a conversation with a complete stranger, even though it didn't feel that way, and how funny it was that he was so interested in what I was doing on Christmas. And he then shared with me what he was going to do. He was also the first person, in a very long time outside my family and friends, to wish me a Merry Christmas.

I suddenly felt so good. A warm feeling of joy and unity arose. It didn't seem like I was talking with a stranger, but a close friend I met again. His smile and our conversation truly demonstrated the concept of Oneness. That there are no strangers or others. That we all want happiness, free from suffering. There was no concept of "who is that stranger?"

I was a bit shocked as to how this simple, yet profound, moment had affected me.

We never know how we will affect those around us. Even a simple smile can bring about great joy and change within one.

For me, this is what the holidays are all about. Sharing a kind moment, or sharing a warm smile with others. To treat all as if they were a part of your family.

Especially to those whom we call "strangers." The exchange of compassion, as opposed to material goods.

So, I told my family this story and told them that this moment, for me, was a true holiday gift.

SKIPPING ROCKS
Michael Shinyo Lawrence

As a child, I enjoyed skipping rocks across the water whenever we visited a pond or lake. It would often become a competition with my siblings to see how far we could skip a rock or how many times it would skip before either sinking or reaching the other side. If your rock reached the other side, you automatically won. Part of the experience involved finding the right skipping rock. It had to be flat and fit well along the index finger. Launching it had to be done at the right angle for it to bounce off the surface of the water, and it had to have enough force behind it to keep going.

When a rock is found, it does not think of itself as a skipping rock. This is a label we give it. The rock has a nature of stillness and calmness. Every time a rock is skipped across the water, it creates ripples at every point it impacts. These ripples spread and touch other ripples and eventually touch the entire body of water to some extent. This is much like our daily lives. Our intentions, speech, and actions cause ripples too. It is difficult to have compassionate intentions *and* speak or act with wisdom. Often, our speech or actions are a response to an emotion. We may have right intention, yet not realize that our speech is divisive. This is an example of compassion without wisdom. This is where right mindfulness comes in. Before reacting, contemplate what is going on physically with the body, what emotions you are experiencing, what thoughts come to mind, or if these thoughts are true. Rumors are a good example of this. Any given day, you can look on Facebook and read something that sparks an emotion. Many times, what is read is based on another's reaction to an emotion. This is the first skipping of the rock. Then, we react and either comment or share that post and the rock skips again. All this time, more ripples are made. Many times, these ripples continue and are lacking in truth.

A rock can also give historical clues. Certain minerals and fossils can give some idea as to what types of plants and animals lived in an area before. They can even show us a little about erosion. Think of these clues as memories.

Before skipping a rock, or reacting, meditate with it. What happened to cause an emotion that you feel requires a reaction? Thinking of the rock as a neutral party, what facts might it see? What is your motivation for skipping the rock? Tell the rock the same message you wish to tell others. What kind of ripples do you think this will make? Contemplate how those ripples will affect others. Will skipping the rock make you feel better? After sitting with your rock, decide to either skip the rock across your pond or just be like the rock. What memories of an event or reaction do you want to keep?

DHARMA IS EVERYWHERE
Jeff Wayo Ward

Beating Robin's wings
Cuts nature's silent passing
The world speaks Dharma

Warm air awakens
The red sky breaks horizon
Splendid is Dharma

Golden falls decay
The pumpkin spice lingers
Eternal Dharma

Ice wind cuts deeply
The temple walls a relief
My refuge Dharma

Just a poetic reminder that the Dharma is everywhere, it is brilliant in its teachings, it lasts forever, and it gives shelter to the spirit.

FEELING FULL
Shaku Sayo Shenphen

Ever feel full after a meal? Like it was the best meal you ever had? Or when you just had the greatest Thanksgiving day feast and have the feeling of complete satisfaction. For me, this is the feeling I like to develop every day and every moment.

I want to always feel full of life and full with life. A deep sense of complete satisfaction. To be so thankful for having everything I need that I feel nothing more is needed. To be completely full.

More and more I have been appreciating how full I am feeling. Contented by all the gifts of universal life. I'm thankful for the many causes and conditions, all the people, and all the things that come together to allow me to be full and alive in every moment.

Being full is a practice of being grateful. A sense that nothing is missing as I freely flow in the Great Ocean of Universal life. To be beyond dualisms and labels. To be full of spirit, wisdom, and compassion.

Full is Oneness. It is a mind fully blessed by the present where nothing is needed and all has been attained. Knowing that life will unfold as it should without ego, free of conceptions and misleading ideas.

Be thankful and full now like life is feeding you a banquet every moment. Be full and never feel hungry again.

STAGE FRIGHT
Morris Sekiyo Sullivan

I got an email, one day, inviting me to provide an invocation for an upcoming County Commission meeting. Of course I was happy to accept the invitation. But when I started to approach the podium, I realized I was nervous—I had a little stage fright.

I should mention that for much of my adult life, I was terrified of public speaking. It was a hindrance, so I worked at overcoming it. These days, I give a lot of formal and informal sermons, dharma talks, and classroom talks. So talking about the dharma -- well, that's one of the things I do a lot and enjoy doing.

To discover I was nervous was kind of a surprise. I'm sure I could find a reason for my anxiety. I was outside my usual comfort zone; I was in a jacket and tie instead of robes; I was in front of a group of people who might not be friendly toward Buddhists, etc., etc. But it really doesn't matter why -- I was anxious, and that was the circumstance within which I needed to function.

Later that week, I arrived for my weekly meeting at the chapel of a state correctional institution. It was early afternoon, and the chapel's air conditioning was not working. I'm in Florida, and it's very hot this time of year. The chapel was like a sauna. There are windows in the sanctuary, but the chaplain was conferring with a corrections officer and the administration, and so far it seemed that, for some reason, the windows probably could not be opened.

As you can imagine, inmates were complaining about the heat. Some speculated about how the air conditioner got broken or were looking for people to blame for that, or griping about the unfairness of having to keep the windows closed. None of that speculating, griping or blaming made it any cooler.

One of the inmates, a former armed robber who became an ordained Soto Zen monk while incarcerated, was reminded of the famous discourse between a monk and Master Tōzan. The monk wanted to know how to avoid cold and heat.

Tōzan answered, "Why don't you go to the place where there is no cold or heat?"

The monk asked, "Where is that place?"

Tōzan said, "When it is cold, let it be so cold it kills you. When hot, let it be so hot it kills you."

This doesn't mean that to escape the heat you should go meditate in Death Valley until you get heatstroke or in Antarctica until you get hypothermia. It means to go to that place in your heart where you accept the present moment as it is. The "you" that is killed is that "you" that insists that heat not be hot and cold not be cold.

The conditions of heat and cold might come from the environment, but "being hot" and "being cold" come from within. It's the same with nervousness—there might be causes "out there," but the anxiety is "in here." So this is counter-intuitive, but the way to deal with performance anxiety is to be so nervous it kills you -- to let go of that "self" that insists that there be no anxiety. In other words, go ahead and feel nervous, and do what you're there to do.

When you accept anxiety, you don't get nervous about being nervous, and you're able to go ahead and do what you need to do. So when I gave that invocation, I don't think anyone besides me noticed I was nervous. I got some nice feedback from commissioners -- and they asked me back, so I must have done okay.

That day at the prison chapel, we accepted the heat, we started our service, and we meditated. About 10 minutes into our first meditation, I felt a breeze. The administration had given the chapel clerks the go-ahead to open the windows. We were still in Florida and it was still July, so this was not a particularly cool breeze. But I have to tell you, when you're in that place where it's so hot it kills you, even a warm, humid breeze feels pretty darn good.

SEE THE NOW
Jeff Wayo Ward

"I am Buddha" stated my three year old the other day without provocation or any lead up. Just out of the blue and quite matter-of-factly. Now he is only three so I haven't discussed metaphysical issues with him such as Buddha Nature or how each sentient being is a potential Buddha. Right now the definition of the word potential may be a bit outside his vocabulary. But there he was just singing and dancing, being a kid when he suddenly stopped looked up and made this profound statement then went right back to playing without missing a beat. I mean who knows how much more of the universe a child understands before we set the weight of the world upon those little shoulders.

A child truly sees the world with such wonderment and joy. His little cherubic face lights up and radiates joy at something as simple as a butterfly or bird in flight. It is amazing how the "little things" mean so much to him. The other day he found a box of crayons that had been pushed to the back of the drawer on his fisher-price desk and it was "daddy, daddy LOOK what I found" with such excitement. I thought it must be incredible to see the world through those eyes. Right then I made decision to try and make a conscious effort on occasion to look at the world with child-like wonderment. On the way to work this morning it was snowing, but rather then grumble I set aside my adult eyes and saw the snow as he would, it was a truly beautiful sight, quite thrilling a blanket of pure white that made me crack a smile. My advice to everyone is to take a moment every now and then to examine the world through your inner-child, embrace that remnant of innocence and laugh out loud. That is my Dharma Glimpse.

HEADING TOWARD THE SUN
Shaku Sayo Shenphen

We all have a destination. Mine is to head toward the Sun. Light has always represented wisdom, compassion, enlightenment.

My Dharma name, *Sayo*, means Swift Sun. *Yo*, or Sun, is part of the Dharma name given to all those who form part of the Bright Dawn lineage, or family. We are all part of the Sun.

As I travel through life, the Sun is my guide.

As life begins the end, the Sun will shine the path to peace.

So my destination is clear as the light of day.

I am heading toward the Sun!

A BUDDHIST TOOLBOX
Toyo T. Katamori

The toolbox. Everyone has one, or two, conveniently within reach, to allow the proper fixing of just about everything at home or at a friend's house. Toolboxes are in every person's life, no matter if they don't know how to use what's in them. There are many types of toolboxes: some larger, and more elaborate than others. But it's not the size or elaborateness that counts; it is what's in the toolbox that really is most important. These are the tools in the toolbox, and they are chosen because of the application they serve. These tools are our servants and serve our needs. Sometimes they need to be borrowed by our buddies and friends. There are always the basic tools in the box, and common tools, like screw drivers, hammers, rulers, squares, levels, and plumbs. In many cases there is a special tool in there, one that was only used once or twice, and cost the most; however it had gotten the job done.

There is another toolbox which you will not find in the shed or garage. It is a Buddhist's toolbox. It is stored apart, unseen and within. It is our toolbox that so many have. It is now loaded with tools, full to the top. These tools are so different in comparison, but all have the same type of results. In the end not everyone really knows how many tools they even have, not to forget to mention how to use the tools in there. Many have used tools by accident and didn't realize until later. Some are neglected and turn rusty over time. How many times do we as Buddhist go to the toolbox looking for that right tool? As we develop in our Dharma, we have learned through practice which tool is right for a particular job. We still screw it up, but we work it out with another tool and eventually make it right. We struggle as we open up the toolbox and find it at its capacity.

We find usages for our tools. We bring them to the Sangha, a work shop for Dharma tools.

These tools we have were given to us by the Buddha, our teacher. He is the teacher and has provided us with the knowledge of tools. The Dharma is the teachings, and they are the tools in our toolbox. The Sangha is the taught and the workshop where we use our tools. There are three major tools in our Buddhist Toolbox that are most important to our Dharma. They are the Square, Level, and the Plumb. These are old tools and have been around since the Neolithic period. Once designed, time was invented. Buildings were erected and roads were laid across our world. But for Buddhist these tools, Square, Level, and the Plumb are old as well. Many fraternal societies over time used these same tools and all adapted their own meanings and relations to comparisons.

The Level is the Three Treasures, using the Buddha in the middle to balance the ends which the Sangha and the Dharma are perched. Without these three coinciding with one another, the level does not show true. A Buddhist acts on the Level and conducts themselves in a level state in all transaction in Nature. The Buddha is the teacher, the Dharma is the Teachings, and the Sangha is the Taught.

The Square is the Four Noble Truths. The square is the fourth part of a circle in which is Oneness. The square put to work that as it is used to give four equal proportions so the level and the plume show true.

1. The Noble Truth of the reality of Dukkha as part of conditioned existence.
2. The Noble Truth that Dukkha has a causal arising.
3. The Noble Truth of the end of Dukkha,
4. The Noble Truth of the Path that leads to Awakening.

The Plumb is the Eight Fold Path, and is worked in such a way that it exemplifies 8 degrees of the Dharma: Right Speech, Right View, Right Thought, Right Action, Right Livelihood, Right Effort, Right Mindfulness, and Right Mediation. As we pass through the Dharma, sometimes we are not level and our actions not square and we need to focus on which degree of the plumb we are standing.

There are other tools that we use after checking our work for Level, Square and Plumb. The hammer, screw driver, ruler, pliers, and scissors are also in our Buddhist toolbox. These five tools can be related to the five precepts.

1. Abstain from killing living beings
2. Abstain from taking that which not given
3. Abstain from sexual misconduct
4. Abstain from false speech
5. Abstain from distilled substances that confuse the mind. (Alcohol and Drugs). However they are not defined as the Square, Level and Plumb, which allows all of us to decide which precept is matched with these five subordinate tools in our Buddhist tools box. Although one fact remains certain, they all are Anicca — Impermanent and need to be replaced with anew and all are interdependent of one another. So take care of those tools, and every now and then start a project in which you will need to use a Square, Level and Plumb in your Buddhist Toolbox.

SPIDERWORT
Morris Sekiyo Sullivan

Previously published in *Oneness—Quarterly Newsletter of Bright Dawn Institute for American Buddhism*

Every year around this time, my front yard begins to bloom with spiderwort. Native plant enthusiasts might argue otherwise, but a spiderwort is pretty much a weed. I like them, though, because their blooms range from electric blue to violet and have bright yellow anthers. They also attract butterflies and fat black-and-yellow bumblebees. I have tried to cultivate spiderworts in flowerbeds alongside more domesticated flowers -- I've tried transplanting them and even buying potted ones at the annual Native Plant Society sale. However, they seem determined to grow anywhere except where I want them.

I once discussed spiderworts with the pastor of a nearby historic Baptist church. I admitted a little sheepishly that I put off the first spring mowing of my lawn as long as possible so I could enjoy their blooms. He admitted he did the same thing. We agreed that if nothing else it was nice to have an excuse to avoid mowing the lawn.

Like spiderworts, the dharma doesn't always show itself where you want or expect it. You might sit down on your meditation cushion to "listen" for a teaching to arise from your peaceful heart yet hear nothing but noise, or travel to a grand dharma center for a retreat with a famous teacher and learn nothing. And then there you are on the treadmill at the gym, in the checkout line at the grocery store or in your front yard, and you come face to face with Universal Truth.

I've been interested in Buddhism much of my life. However, my practice was on-again off-again and I really didn't "self-identify," as the pollsters call it, as "a Buddhist" until about eight years ago. When my wife and I began sitting with a fledgling meditation group, I reawakened a practice that had lain dormant for a while. I enjoyed meditating and reading about the dharma, but I can't say I was getting a lot out of it until one morning, when I walked Faust, who was still a puppy then.

My neighborhood goes from suburban to rural, a few blocks west of my house, where the sidewalk ends and cow pastures begin. Along one stretch, Spanish bayonets grow right next to the street, so the dog and I have to walk in the road there. There's usually not much traffic in the morning, so drivers will move over to give us room to walk without having to get scraped and skewered by the dagger-like leaves.

The road was clear, but as Faust and I reached a point where the growth was at its thickest, a pickup came over a hill and toward us. I expected the driver to drift toward his left -- there was no other traffic, so he could easily do that.

However, he came closer and closer, hugging the shoulder, until the last minute when I yanked on the leash and pulled Faust into the Spanish bayonet with me.

I stared dumbfounded at the driver as he passed. I could see him gripping his wheel, scowling as he passed, as if to say we should stay the heck out of his street! I was so angry -- I couldn't believe the lack of consideration, the outright meanness of this jackass, this stupid old jerk, this --

...and as I turned to watch him pass, perhaps to shout at him as he drove away, I saw the sun over the crest of the next hill, its bright morning rays shining right into my eyes so that I could see neither the truck nor anything else on the road. This poor guy -- whom I had deemed a scowling, inconsiderate jackass -- had been blinded by the sun that had just peered over the horizon. He hadn't even seen us as he squinted into the sun, trying to keep his vehicle under control.

I felt deflated. I had come face-to-face with my anger and with the realization how far off the mark had flown my mental fabrications -- my assumptions and intentions about the driver of the pickup. It left me feeling slightly nauseous. But at the same time, the true importance of my Buddhist practice dawned on me.

I once heard a weed defined as "a plant for which no one has yet discovered a use." Of course, we shouldn't cultivate anger -- we'd better yank it up by the roots and cultivate more skillful emotional states. But once in a while, perhaps even anger can point us toward important knowledge about our true nature.

A few weeks ago, I noticed the spiderwort is especially prolific this year. For whatever reason, when the grass got high enough to start looking shaggy, the patches of spiderwort had gotten thicker than ever, the plants taller than I remembered them being in the past.

It occurred to me that flowerbeds should be where the flowers grow, and not the other way around. I got the lawnmower out of the shed and carefully began mowing around my new spiderwort garden.

EVERYDAY IS A HOLIDAY
Shaku Sayo Shenphen

One morning, during my ministry training program, I prepared to upload a Dharma Glimpse and report, only to discover that my computer had suffered a major crash. Even as I wrote the report, I was wondering how I could recover my system. I searched around for the needed disks in hopes that they may be able to fix the problem. Without a solution to this issue, I would not be able to recover both my report and glimpse.

I took a moment to pause. Actually, I took a moment to laugh at the situation. Instead of "this always happens to me", I laughed and actually said, "I'm glad this happened to me". It made me feel alive. When problems arise, I feel they are good moments to put the Dharma to work. Even though I knew that I would have to rewrite my report and glimpse, this situation broke me out of my usual Sunday schedule. Now I had to change my schedule around and try to rewrite my glimpse and report.

I took another moment of pause. This time I decided to relax for a moment and listen to a record I had found. The record was from the musical *Mame*. This musical and movie have always been, at least to me, very inspirational. My favorite line in the musical/movie, is one spoken by the main character, Mame Dennis:

"Live, live, live…
Life's a banquet and most poor
sons of bitches are starving to death!"

This line always makes me laugh at my problems. So I have always kept it in mind, especially in times of trouble. Then, I decided to watch the movie version, starring Lucille Ball. In the first scene Mame and her guest are celebrating. When asked by a guest: "Mame, what the hell are we celebrating?", she response, "A holiday! One I just invented". Then she continued to sing the song: "It's Today". These are the opening lyrics:

Light the candles,
Get the ice out,
Roll the rug up,
It's today.
Though it may not be any one's birthday,
And though it's far from the first of the year,
I know that this very minute has history in it, we're here!

And this made me think that today is a holiday, not Christmas or Hanukah, but my own Computer Crash Day!

I celebrated and rejoiced in this new idea. So much so that I stopped thinking about the computer issue, and was inspired to write this new Dharma Glimpse.

Mame is right. Every day should be a Holiday. Why? "We're here!" Do we really need any other excuse to celebrate life to the fullest? To enjoy the present…. Do we need special or government sanctioned holidays to rejoice and celebrate? NO! We should celebrate everyday like it was a holiday…. Your *special* Holiday.

So when life gets you down, your computer crashes, plans are not working out like you wanted, stop for a moment and celebrate your own Holiday! Because this very minute has history in it… and we're here!

DHARMA TIME
Jeff Ward

Dharma Time
Without End
Seems to pass
Without notice

That which was
Eternal
Is now Ephemeral

A ghost of what was
Cast a shade on
What is to be

In twilight time
The Truth
Dims the fire
Of desire's passion

Tranquility is an
Ocean of Life
Time without envy
So passes this day
Into the next
An unbroken chain
Of Emptiness.

The first stanza is meant to reflect the Absolute Universe as a Wheel, one without beginning or end. The second stanza refers to how the relative/conceptual world is illusionary. The third stanza is Karmic Law and how the choices we make flavor the present moment and our future. The fourth stanza is how through meditation and self reflection the Dharma can come to quell our clinging. The final stanza reflects peace in the ocean (Oneness) of all life and the acceptance of Sunyata.

INTERNET MINDFULNESS: PRACTICING IN THE 21ST CENTURY AND BEYOND!

Shaku Sayo Shenphen

Many of us today are unable to dedicate much time to sitting meditation. We come home after a hard day at work and the last thing we think about is going to our S.P.O.T. *(Special Place Of Tranquility)* and sitting for five or ten minutes. Most of us tend to quickly log on to the Internet to check our emails or to chat with friends and family. There is nothing wrong with that. But we can turn these activities into one of mindfulness and awareness. Yes, the Internet can be a great spiritual tool!

We live in an Internet world. We get our news from the net. We send letters and communicate through chats and forums. When we get on the net, we should do it fully aware and present in the Eternal Now. As Gyomay Sensei mentions in his texts, when we do something, we should do it a hundred percent! When blogging, only blog. When sending emails, simply focus on what you're typing. Nothing more. In this way you are being aware, mindful. You are meditating.

Some people worry that they cannot visit a local temple or Sangha to learn Dharma because they live too far away from one. But thanks to the Internet we can hear Dharma right from our computers. We can download teachings to listen to and reflect on. A great example of this would be the Bright Dawn Online Sangha. Using the Bright Dawn Ning[1] site can be a very powerful, spiritual tool. One can listen to past Dharma teachings by Koyo Sensei and Dharma glimpses from members of the Bright Dawn Sangha. You can also watch Koyo Sensei's fun "Sensei Says" youtube videos. There are also blogs from members that we can read. We can even set up time to chat with other Bright Dawn Sangha members.

Blogging and sharing blog posts can also be a spiritual tool and practice. If you had a rough day at work . . . blog about it! Through the actual practice of blogging we release a lot of our afflictive emotions, daily frustrations, and tensions. We begin to see our issues through a different angle. And by writing things out we spend time reflecting on that particular situation, whether happy or sad. We may even inspire others through what we write, our situation, and how we learned from them. Sharing and expressing are very good ways to engage in spiritual practice and awareness.

It is for these reasons that I personally love and enjoy visiting the Bright Dawn Ning site/online Sangha. Visiting the site is like spending time in meditation, in reflection. As I write my blogs I see things differently. It is a source of inspiration. Also, sharing our stories and teachings is exactly the main function of a Sangha. I can also play recordings from past Live Dharma Sunday broadcasts. Listening to them more than once allows me to get a different perspective every time.

So, the next time you're on the computer, on the Internet, be sure to put some of these ideas into practice and see what comes up. Be fully aware and One with those moments.

[1] www.brightdawnsangha.ning.com

Bright Dawn Dharma Glimpses:

LAY MINISTER CLASS
#4

"GASSHO"
Doug Kuyo Slaten

A few weeks ago while at work I had a surprising and pleasant experience which I think could be called a Dharma Glimpse. I mean, after all, what isn't?

Like so many of the opportunities for spiritual growth that are presented to me, this one involved driving. This time, though, I wasn't on the soul-destroying freeways of Los Angeles but rather in one of the parking garages at LAX. I don't work for the airport but my office happens to be located there.

I was leaving for home spiraling my way down to the exit in parking structure #5. The outside track which I was on intersects with the parking aisles as you go down and you have to be careful about cars suddenly appearing as you round a corner. People often drive too fast in these structures even though visibility is limited and there are travelers milling about and not paying attention. I don't know why it is, maybe they're in a hurry or tired or in a bad mood, but I've learned that I need to be alert to drivers coming into the exit lane fast and without looking, which is exactly what happened. In this case the other car was being driven by a burly-looking gentleman with a shaved head who I don't think was a monk and there was an older man in the front passenger seat who may have been his father.

The driver, who was scowling, stopped in time to avoid T-boning me (I stopped as well) and then made an angry and impatient gesture with his hand signifying that I should be the one to continue on. I get this imperious wave from time to time, usually at 4-way stops where there are well-established rules of the road but the other driver decides to play traffic cop. The rude gesture in this case prompted me to roll down my window and I was about to mouth the words, "I-had-the-right-of-way" pausing for a moment to decide if I should tack on an expletive.

As we eyeballed each other waiting to see how this was going to go, something totally unexpected happened. Instead of delivering my prepared remarks I kept my mouth shut and then of their own volition my hands came up together in "gassho." Even more surprising was the reaction of the two men in the other car, as their faces relaxed and they also spontaneously raised their hands not exactly in gassho but in a likewise conciliatory gesture to imply that my message of peace was received.

I proceeded on my way to the exit and in my rearview mirror I could see the other car now being driven slowly and carefully behind me. The good feeling I got from this experience stayed with me for quite a while. And perhaps equally important was that I de-fused a potentially angry confrontation. I know from experience that if I give in to anger I pay the price physically and emotionally. My whole mood deteriorates and I feel separated from everybody and everything. Sure, I tell and re-tell the story, gradually polishing it to make my behavior seem not only justified but necessary, but even if I can force others to agree with me there is no real satisfaction. Eventually I am only left with regret and the small consolation that life will surely provide me with another opportunity at which time I can perhaps behave more skillfully.

Since my gassho was the key action in this episode I looked up the meaning of this gesture. The sites that popped up from my Google search were in basic agreement that gassho implies recognition of the oneness of all beings and is used variously to express respect, prevent scattering of the mind, unify dualities, bring the self into dynamic balance and to express the One Mind - the unity of being.

Now, all of this can be understood on an intellectual level, but during the experience I have related there was no thought. For a moment, my ego-driven small mind was over-ridden by something more intuitive, and with one unconscious gesture I tapped into those spiritual resources of gassho that I just listed. I felt like someone presented with a koan where an immediate, non-analytical response is required. I'm a little worried since I can't be sure that I won't go back to my bad old ways the next time a similar situation presents itself, but for now I am grateful for having been given this lesson.

THE GOLDEN RULE
Seiyo Thomas DeMann

The main thrust of the Theravadin Buddhist tradition is to follow the original teachings of the Buddha. One of the important original teachings concerns Loving-kindness. The Metta Sutta explains how significant and important the Buddha felt this principle is.

I would like to start with four quotes by the Dalai Lama who comes from a completely different tradition.

The Dalai Lama has been quoted as saying, "My religion is very simple. My religion is kindness". Dalai Lama has also said, "This is my simple religion. There is no need for temples; no need for complicated philosophy. Our own brain, our own heart is our temple; the philosophy is kindness." The Dalai Lama also said, "Whether one believes in a religion or not, and whether one believes in rebirth or not, there isn't anyone who doesn't appreciate kindness and compassion." The very last quote that I have to share from the Dalai Lama is, "Our main purpose in this life is to help others. If you cannot help them, at least do not hurt them."

All of these quotes relate the same message which is the Golden Rule; do unto others as you would like them to do unto you. Treat others as you would like to be treated yourself. Who does not want kindness directed toward him or herself?

In the March 2011 issue of the Shambhala Sun, Karen Armstrong wrote an article that the magazine paraphrased as: Why the Golden Rule is the key to humanity's future. The Golden Rule is best known as a Christian principle but I feel that is it important to all of us. Karen relates to us in her article a true story of a famous Jewish Rabbi by the name of Rabbi Hillel. As the story goes, the Rabbi was approached by a pagan who promised to convert to Judaism if the Rabbi was able to recite the whole Jewish teaching while standing on one leg. Rabbi Hillel stood on one leg and said, "That which is hateful to you, do not do to your neighbor. That is the Torah; everything else is only commentary. Go and study it." Many of the things that we think essential to Judaism, such as the unity of God, the creation of the world, the exodus from Egypt, the 613 commandments, they're all commentary on the Golden Rule. Go study it, said Rabbi Hillel; make it your reality. It is my feeling that this also is very true of Buddhism. Take a look at the Five Precepts… aren't they commentaries on how to treat others correctly? The Eightfold Path instructs us to be Right in our actions… more commentary! The Dhammapada, the sayings of the Buddha, is also a book of commentary.

In the same article Karen spoke about Confucius, who lived 500 years before Jesus. Confucius was asked by his disciples, "Master, which of your teachings can we put into practice all day and every day? What is the central thread that runs through all your teachings?" Confucius advised to look into your own heart, discover what gives you pain, and then refuse under any circumstance to inflict that pain on anybody else.

Karen said that when religious leaders get together they get into many lively discussions about current issues but compassion usually isn't one of the topics. To quote Karen, "With their teachings on the Golden Rule, it seems to me that religions should be playing a major role in one of the chief tasks of our times, which is to build a global community in which people of all persuasions can live together in peace, harmony and respect. If we don't achieve that, it's unlikely in this age of global terror that we'll have a viable world to hand on to the next generation".

There is one Universal Truth that ties everything and all the teachings together. This Truth reveals what we are, why we are here and how to act. In listening to the Buddha, Jesus, the Dalai Lama, Rabbi Hillel and Confucius, perhaps we have discovered this Truth: "I will try my best to treat others as I would like to be treated myself".

A Zen Master relates that the meaning of Buddhism is: Do No Evil, Only Do Good and keep the mind clean and clear. One of the Master's disciples says that even a child of 7 years knows this. The Master agrees that a child of 7 does in fact know this but that a man of 70 finds this impossible to do.

We may have discovered the Universal Truth. Are we already aware of the Truth but find it impossible to do like the Zen Master said?

Now what do we do with it?

Rabbi Hillel said to go study it and make it our reality.

HOSPICE TRAINING
Marilyn Chiyo

During volunteer training for our local hospice some ten years ago, I participated in an exercise I will never forget. We were each given a stack of blank cards to label. On each of four cards, we were told to write an activity or hobby we particularly enjoyed. On one card, we wrote our current job or vocation. On three cards, we wrote physical activities or sports we enjoyed. On five cards, we wrote the names of five loved ones. Three cards were labeled with something we enjoyed from nature.

The staff then began to tell us that growing old, getting frail or infirm and approaching death or a terminal illness, involves letting go very consciously. If we were to work with hospice patients, we would need to understand, on a deeper, level what the process feels like.

We laid our cards out on the table in front of us – a mini collection of our lives. There in front of me were the names of my mother, my husband, our daughters, and my brother, the job I loved, my hobbies, sports, the ocean, a breeze on my face, the green of summer.

The exercise began with a story we were to imagine about ourselves. An illness put us in the hospital for observation and tests. The news was not good. Facing a debilitating and terminal illness, we decided to quit our job and make the most of whatever health we might enjoy. We each gave the card with our jobs to a staffer who collected them.

Our energy waned and we were not able to participate in a couple of the physical activities we had enjoyed. We were asked to select two more cards to give to the staffer. So far, the exercise didn't seem so bad. We had a lot of cards and could select which ones to give up. I didn't snow ski much anymore anyway, so giving up that card was easy.

As the story went on, however, staffers would come around and take away a card or two without our permission. The story was getting sad, and we didn't like having the cards of things we enjoyed taken from us. The light-heartedness started to leave the room.

As we approached death in the story, people we loved were taken from us. We had to pick the cards of loved ones who would precede us in death. Uneasily, I picked my mother and then my brother. A staffer came by and picked the card of my husband. A lump formed in my throat.

We were down to very few cards by now. The names of my daughters and a breeze on my face were staring at me from the table in front of me. The staffer came by and asked for the cards of my daughters. With tears in my eyes, I refused to give them up. "I don't play these games with my children", I recall saying as I picked up the cards labeled with their names, and put them in my pocket.

There was one card left: the breeze on my face. Finally, I gave that one up.

Ten years later, my mother is now dead. I spent the day with my eldest daughter, selecting a formal she will wear next Saturday to the prom with her boyfriend. The girls have grown up so fast. My husband and I are enjoying our family as though this precious time will go on forever. In my heart, I still want to put the cards with their names into my pocket and keep them safe. I know I cannot.

My Buddhist practice is slowly forming. With Bright Dawn I selected a mantra, "This is a worthy moment". It is a helpful mantra for me, one that honors the wondrous moments in my day, and helps me pause and honor the difficult moments. But I see now that it is insufficient. I must expand my mantra. What do you think?

This is a worthy moment.

Let it go.

HUSBAND IN ER
Patti Kayo

A couple of days ago, my husband left for work around 5:30 a.m. for his hour-and-a-half long, morning, L.A. commute. When he called me 45 minutes later saying he was in the hospital, I feared the worst. All he could tell me is that he had had some sort of episode while driving, went to the hospital, and they were working him up.

When your stressed-out 63-year-old husband calls you from the ER, it gets your attention. I knew I wanted to be there and *fast*. The hospital he was in, was about 45 miles away, and when I left the house, traffic was in full bloom -- complete gridlock on the 101 and 405 freeways.

At first, I panicked thinking about not being able to get there, and having no clue what my husband was going through, or if he was even alive by now. I tried every lane. It seemed I kept choosing the wrong lane, so I'd switch to another one only to find myself losing ground (using some truck as a marker). Every time I insinuated myself into another lane and gave an apologetic wave to the perturbed person I just moved in front of, I'd be greeted by angry gestures and honks. I was frantic, and all my clever maneuvering was only getting me further behind.

I turned on the radio for help. Yep, confirmed, all freeways are a mess. I knew I would eventually get there, maybe 2 or 3 hours from now, but I wanted to be there, right *now*. It should only be a 45-minute drive. My husband knows all the ins and outs of the residential streets and canyon roads along this route, but I do not. I determined that I would have to stay on the freeway, as bad as it was, or I'd surely get lost and make matters worse.

Of course, there was no way to contact my husband, to let him know I'm on the way, and that I was just stuck in traffic. And there was no way for me to know if he was okay, or find out what he was going through. I was wishing I could have a sign on my car announcing that my need is greater than all of yours, let me through for gosh sakes! Special consideration here!

But how could the other drivers know of my desperation? I looked like every other crazed commuter on the road. From inside my car bubble, I felt that all these people were separate from me, different than I am. It was me against them.

I resigned to staying on the path that I knew for certain would get me there, and since there was nothing I could do about the overwhelming circumstances, I told myself to calm down and stop fighting it so that I myself, don't cause more harm. Go with the flow, even when it's slow.

Powerlessness is a good teacher. It forces you to accept your reality. I realized I had to accept things as they were. I took a deep breath, and in the release of my struggle, sitting there stopped on the freeway, embedded amongst thousands of cars, I looked around me and wondered who else was in trouble out there? Who else was feeling lost and desperate?

Stuck in traffic, uncertain of my husband's condition, I came to think that this stream of traffic was a lot like the stream of life, sometimes full of uncertainty and misery. I had as little control over my own, or my husband's destiny, as I did the stream of traffic. I had to surrender myself to the reality and enter the stream. I wasn't an exception to these commuters, I was a part of them. Like it or not, I was even interconnected and interdependent with them. They didn't know it, but I was depending on each one of them to do a good job driving so that I could get to my destination; they were depending on me not to go crazy and impede their journey.

We often feel separate, but we are truly interwoven and interdependent, moving in and out of each other's lanes. All of our actions and decisions affect every other person, and we all have the power to help, or hinder, each other's journey.

The next time I'm in rush-hour traffic and I see someone driving as erratically and seemingly haphazardly as I had been that morning, I'm going to tell myself that maybe they've got a loved one in the ER that needs them to get there. I'll feel kindness rather than annoyance for them and give them a little more space and a one-handed Gassho.

And the best news is that my husband is still here to continue our journey -- together!

RIGHT UNDERSTANDING
Andy Goyo Bondy

I wish I had the exact reference, but I seem to recall reading a koan that essentially said, "If you want it, you've already lost it." While I don't claim to fully understand this nor any other koan, it leads me to remember something essential -- wanting is not the same as having. As long as you want something, you don't have it, and thus it is as good as lost. If you have it, why would you want it? While this can apply to things, it also applies to personal traits -- as long as I want to be noble, humble, kind, even happy, etc., I'm not. And the moment I recognize that I have those qualities, the wanting ceases.

As part of my daily review of Right Understanding, I've extended thinking about how this issue relates to so many aspects of daily life. For example: it seems that if you *think* you've lost something, you must still want it.

That lead to, "If you *think* you own it, it owns you." This is true for objects and people. If I cling to possessing things -- including my 'possessions' -- then that clinging is ruling my life. I am not free if I want to own something -- that thing then has power over me. In a relationship with someone -- whether spouse or children -- as long as one thinks, 'She's mine', then she owns you -- the possession of her controls you and your choices. We can be within a partnership without any ownership at issue -- 'we are married' rather than 'she is *my* wife.' If my happiness is directly tied to the things I own, then their loss will diminish my life. Having a comfortable car to drive is nice, but if I end up driving a 'lesser' car, I will be just as content. My visiting children, from the UK, used our car to go to Philly for a birthday dinner, and returned with a dent in the rear fender. My wife was aghast and angry with them -- my immediate reaction was, these things sometimes happen when anyone drives into Philly and I'll need some time to go fix it. I didn't feel something I owned was marred.

Related to this theme is, "If you *think* you deserve it, it's already deserted you." Let's face it- at times we all think we deserve something -- either an object, an event, or just recognition from someone else. But the moment you go down that path, dukkha is there first, just grinning at you. We virtually never feel that we get the reinforcement we deserve, and while factually what you do get may not be in proportion to your efforts and accomplishments, it is the expectation that produces the first wave of dukkha. Then, when the outcome doesn't quite match the expectation -- not enough, not good enough, not precise enough -- the other waves hit over and over. Because we enjoy praise, we become conditioned to expecting it. This is the contingent nature of the world. It is the calming of the expectation, rather than refraining from doing things within the world, or withdrawing from the world, that is the hard part.

Finally, it dawned on me that, "If I *think* I need it, I'm ignoring what I have." I really need that...car, toy, TV, job, whatever...By focusing on what I don't have -- and thus need -- then I am not in the moment -- I am not recognizing what I already have. I already have a car, many toys, a TV, a job and ...whatever. Many of us eat that second plate of food before our body can even begin to register the first -- we are thus unaware that we already have what we need. And this is repeated all day long -- 'I need...' screams out, compared to the whispered, "I have..."

So, in short...

If you want it, you've already lost it.

If you think you lost it, you still want it.

If you think you own it, it owns you.

If you think you deserve it, it's already deserted you.

And if you think you need it, you're ignoring what you have.

And the Buddha said, I already have it all!

THE BEST DHARMA GLIMPSE – EVER!
David Joyo Merrick

It seems like every few days I say to myself "Oh, that'd make a good Dharma Glimpse." Sometimes I make a note to myself, sometimes not. I started to realize that the more frequent the occurrence, the clearer my path is becoming.

For example, the other day I observed a parent and a young child leaving the gym where they were playing with a basketball. As they left the parent noticed the child looking at the basketball with a smile and she immediately stooped down close to her child and, looking at the ball, said "good bye basketball." And the child repeated it with a smile and wave. This reminded me of the many teachings where "things" were appreciated and thanked.

Another example, this week I received a stomach bug from places unknown. This resulted in my intestinal tract conducting its own flushing and forced me into fasting. I was fortunate that it did not invite Mr. Fever for the event. I immediately thought of Seiyo Thomas-san and his challenges and decided that if there was a way I would make lemonade out of this lemon. Hah! I realized that indeed I did need to lose some weight, and this could be the start. I'd turn this into a weight loss fast and plan to use this time for my stomach (and brain) to get used to the idea that McDonald's was not really comfort food.

It worked. Three days of no food, lots of great liquids, restarting my gut flora using some great yogurts with kick butt probiotics, and I was off and losing. (Oh, and by the way, I did have the initial help of Imodium.)

All that being said, I would rather have initiated a fast on my own terms.

How does all this relate to the "Best Dharma Glimpse – Ever!"?

These are examples of recognizing the Dharma as it is happening, living in the Dharma.

Just as mine is "the best" (each and every one of them…), yours is the best.

The best is the one that is right here – right now.

So, now you know where to find the "Best Dharma Glimpse – Ever!" And you don't even have to Google it.

WHAT A CHANGE
Dave Joyo Merrick

A few days back, my daughter Lily completed an assignment for a group project for her first grade class. One of the things all the kids were assigned to do was to personalize a drawing (color, paint) of a shamrock. Then each child would have a shamrock that they made displayed together with other items.

After Lily completed her shamrock, cut it out and handed it to me, I told her what a great job she did and I casually questioned where she was going to put her name. She looked at me like I was silly and said "why would I want to put my name on it?" I told her "well sweetie, that way everyone will know which one is yours." She calmly looked at me and said, "I know which one is mine…"

Immediately I was enlightened to the teaching. I was attached, I was attached to her getting the credit, and she already was beyond all that. A few years back I would have pressed my point and now I recognize hers.

A BUDDHIST VALENTINE:
"How would the Buddha Love?"
Dave Joyo Merrick

The Sixth Dalai Lama wrote:

*"If one's thoughts towards spirituality were **of** the same **intensity** as **those** towards **love**, one would become a Buddha, in this very body, in this very life."*

Zen Monk: Thay Thich Thong wrote:

Celebrate this day by "Practicing Love and Compassion"
Embrace Valentine's Day as an opportunity to tell friends they are loved and to pay special attention to the people, plants and other things in their lives.

Lama Surya Das wrote:

*Valentine's Day is one of my favorite American holidays. The fact that this heart-centered if over-commercialized day falls around the same time as Tibetan New Year reminds me to make New Year's resolutions relating to those I love and renew my commitment to **cultivating goodness of heart.** These resolutions usually involve opening my heart and mind; listening better; learning to forgive and to love even those I don't like; and coming to accept and bless the world, rather than fighting with it or trying to escape from it.*

As Zen Master Dogen says: "To study the Buddha Way is to be intimate with all things."

Some say we are here in this world to learn and to evolve in consciousness. Certainly primary among life's lessons **is how to love and to love well**, and to **BE** love, as well to give and receive it. I believe love is central to happiness, growth and fulfillment.

How would Buddha love? By seeing every single being, human and otherwise, as fundamentally like himself, and thus able to treat them and love them in the way he would be treated. We call this infinitely benevolent, selfless love, the Awakened Heart, the very spirit of enlightenment.

Buddhist love is based on recognizing our fundamental interconnectedness and knowing that all beings are like ourselves in wanting and needing happiness, safety, fulfillment, and not wanting suffering and misery.

The Dalai Lama says, *"If you want to be wisely selfish, care for others."* All the happiness and virtue in this world comes from selflessness and generosity.

On Valentine's Day, the Dalai Lama's quote of the day on Facebook is: *"All the positive states of mind such as love, compassion, insight and so on, have the quality that you can enhance their capacity and increase their potential to a limitless degree, **if you regularly practice them.**"*

On this Valentine's Day - remember Love is a Verb...

STARLING
Marilyn Chiyo Robinson

I will confess to you that I have a history of difficulty holding my hands together in gassho. To gassho, by putting the palms of both hands together in front of one's heart, is the highest form of respect, symbolizing Oneness. For me, the gesture never felt authentic, like I was an imposter, awkward in the movement, a stand-out convert who was not raised in the tradition. Among other things, this is a story about gassho.

Our youngest daughter spent every spring on what my husband and I called "starling patrols" around our neighborhood. This ritual consisted of walking up and down the sidewalks trying to find and rescue a baby bird before the local cats found it. More than one creature in its death throes has made its way to our home cradled in her t-shirt. None has survived.

Starlings are known locally as trash birds, for their fondness of grain in our agricultural area, and impressive reproductive abilities. But to our daughter, they are wondrous creatures that she watches intently, as herds of them mow our lawn for food each morning. I might add that our daughter is a special child. She is a continual reminder in my life of the beauty of simple kindness.

So it was not surprising when a year and one-half ago, upon arriving home from my book club, my daughter announced she had rescued yet another starling. It was tucked in a box on a towel and put in the shop for the night. And so began her pleading, "please mommy, can I keep her? I've never had a pet of my own, please, please?"

Brief aside, in our defense – we have two dogs, a parrot, hermit crabs, fish, and a toad. It is true that none of the pets are exclusively this daughter's, but they all benefit from her loving attention. So, sure, we felt a little guilty, but not enough to acquire another responsibility. You know when the last one is the last one, right?

Early the next morning, our eldest daughter and I went to the shop to check out the bird. Sure enough, it was a starling, maybe two weeks old, lying on its side with its neck flopping over. Its heart was still beating. "Swell" I thought. At least it would not die alone.

I gently lifted the tiny bird from the towel, cupping it in the length of one hand. As I stood up, I placed my other hand over it for support while carefully taking it into the house. That's when it struck me – my hands were in the gassho position with a beating heart inside. In that moment, I felt compassion well up inside me. I really saw the starling for the first time. This creature had given me a gift.

We are now one and one-half years down the road from that bright dawn morning. I will spare you the details. But I would like to announce the addition to our family of our youngest child's new pet whom she named Olivia, but who has since become Oliver. Oliver is imprinted on me, which is to be expected after nursing him to health hourly for most of his early residence with us. He lives in a large cage given to us by the amused veterinarian who de-wormed him.

Oliver has learned to talk, loves to splash in his bath tub, and eats like a, well, starling. But our daughter loves him and visibly glows with pride as she watches his antics.

I know now that one doesn't really know when the last one is the last one. I suppose it helps to approach life as full of surprises. When we are open to all possibilities, we unconsciously invite the Dharma to enter our lives.

Best of all, for me, gassho will always hold a beating heart.

I gassho to each of you. May each day be full of Bright Dawn moments.

CHANGING VIEW
Douglas Kuyo Slaten

Patti and I are on vacation this week. We are staying in Langley, Washington on Whidbey Island which is in Puget Sound a little north of Seattle. We look forward to these trips because of the beauty and serenity of the area. The stillness and calm is in such contrast to the noise and jangle of Southern California that we have to re-train ourselves to slow down and breathe it in.

The first day we drove the entire length of the island (45 miles) and went out in Skagit County to see the tulips. There is a festival there every Spring and the fields of flowers are a major attraction. The tulips weren't quite ready to bloom but we did see lots of daffodils which were breathtaking against the blue sky and snow-capped mountains.

Our trip got off to a bit of a bumpy start. When we left California on Thursday I was fuming at the perceived mistreatment I was receiving from inept co-workers and uncaring bosses. I was already worrying about an assignment that had been handed to me somewhat unexpectedly and now interfered with my carefully calculated timetable for the future. My usual response in these situations is anger which stems from fear of failure which is actually fear of someone else's disapproval.

So there we were about to go on an all too infrequent trip to a place of rare beauty and serenity and I was already sabotaging any chance at enjoying it. On the ferry ride to the island I was constantly reading my work email on the BlackBerry and forcing Patti to listen to my tirade about how unfair it all was. I am envious of people who can truly enjoy their time off during a vacation. I worry about being behind when I get back to work or missing something "important" when I'm away so I take the job with me wherever I go. Even though I had turned on the "out of office" notice so people got a message that I was on leave, there were still lots of emails from folks who wanted to talk to me even if I was on vacation. If I respond, as I've done in the past, the "vacation" just turns out to be going to work in a different place.

When we arrived in Langley on Thursday night it was dark. The next morning Patti and I went to the window that looks over the Saratoga Passage and were startled at how different the scene was from what we remembered. Winter had turned the landscape barren and through the bare trees we now had a view of the sound and neighboring island that wasn't available the last time we were here. In fact, back then we were thinking of ways to cut down the alders (they are the weed of the Northwest) that were blocking our view. This time we had a different thought. Sometimes during the year the trees block the view and sometimes they don't. The view is always changing. Instead of insisting that it be the same let's enjoy the various moods of the area.

As we started our drive to the Tulip Festival, we talked about that idea as it related to my work. My anxiety and anger were fueled by the unfairness I felt by life handing me something unexpected when I had the future all worked out. Also, all my emotion was being generated from imaginary situations and conversations that were going on in my head. The common theme to these stories was that nothing would ever change once I had defined the intolerable situation. But in reality, just like the view out our window, everything and everybody in the world is constantly changing and that what I perceive is a concerted effort to make me miserable is my mind freezing and attaching itself to a momentary (and probably mistaken) arrangement of events it finds important out of an infinite number of such possibilities.

On the drive I took one phone call and referred the person to my backup team member (I had forgotten to include her name in my "out-of-office" message). Otherwise I didn't look at the blasted thing for the rest of the day, a "personal best" for me.

Capping phrase: The changing view
Code Phrase: Do tomorrow's work tomorrow

LESSONS FROM A MICROWAVE OVEN
Patti Kayo

My Dharma glimpse came to me at about 2 a.m. the other day, when I got up to microwave heat a rice-filled thingy I use for neck pain, something I do just about every night. Like ten thousand times before, it was just me and the microwave in the middle of the night for two minutes on "high."

I've owned this same microwave for 10 years. It's installed above the stove, right at my eye level. And, of course, I use it many times during the day, every day. But this night I became aware, FOR THE FIRST TIME, that it had buttons on it labeled "Popcorn", "Reheat", "Vegetables", and some others. I couldn't believe my eyes. This is a new and exciting feature! Who put those there and when did they do it?

While being amazed and excited at the new microwaving possibilities in my future, the bell dinged, I opened the door, and then I also noticed, FOR THE FIRST TIME, there was a cooking guide inside the door. Say what?? Yes! A cooking guide corresponding to the new buttons on the outside!

I began to wonder how it is that I've been using this machine every day, several times a day, and not seen half of the prominently displayed features? What else is in front of my face that I'm overlooking?

As I wandered back to bed, I wondered when was the last time I actually looked at my family members' faces. What did my daughter wear to school today? How often do I walk past my good people and look through them?

In our reading this week, Stephen Batchelor stated that we are unaware of the extent to which we are distracted because *distraction is a state of unawareness.* My microwave oven is trying to tell me the same thing. Wake up!

It only takes one second to actually look at someone and see them, but in my semi-conscious state I'm missing out on the here and now. If someone were to tell me that I had only another 24 hours to live, you bet I'd be looking at everything and everyone consciously and deliberately—awake!

I can never look at my microwave oven the same now, since it spoke to me, without being reminded to pay attention.

Thank you, honorable microwave.

COMPUTER DHARMA
Douglas Kuyo Slaten

As usual, I didn't have an "aha" experience this week such as Basho describes in his haiku on the deceptively ordinary nazuna wildflower. So my Dharma Glimpse will probably sound a little manufactured or worked-through. There's a Latin expression, *"redolet lucernum"* which literally means "it smells of the lamp" and implies writing which feels labored. To me, that seems like the last impression a Dharma Glimpse should give. But I have a responsibility and a deadline and I can't wait forever for inspiration. So even though I don't personally feel that my report is much of a spiritual insight I'll "keep going" as Rev. Koyo advises us.

Having used up my share of "car and driver" metaphors I thought I'd talk about the other machine which takes up a lot of my time -- the computer. Since I'm practically alone in my office all day, the computer is my interface with the rest of the world and to a large extent dictates my emotional state. When the email in-basket is full of good cheer it makes me happy, but my mood can easily deteriorate when all of a sudden a last-minute Tasker or a flaming arrow from my boss appears. It's funny how much power I let an innocuous screen of text have over me. Without any real knowledge of the mind or mood of the sender I generate a flood of feelings from something practically as devoid of intrinsic meaning as a psychiatrist's ink blot.

But what really strikes me about the behavior of computers is their tendency to freeze up just when you let your guard down. In the past, this has usually meant a loss of data and has been the occasion of some violent outbursts on my part. It doesn't happen so much now since I'm in the habit of saving my work constantly, and also computers are better now about recovering files after a crash.

But every now and then when you're really going good the screen locks up and you realize that no amount of key pounding or mouse clicking is going to bring it back, and your fingers start to hover over the CTRL-ALT-DEL keys. You've resigned yourself to the fact that a "warm" or "soft" re-boot is the only thing that's going to get the screen unstuck. And here, the computer has presented you with a teaching.

In our Lay Ministry Group readings this week from his book "Practicing the Power of Now," Eckhart Tolle, or "ET" as I like to call him says:

"Do not give all your attention away to the mind and the external world. In any thought activity, make it a habit to go back and forth every few minutes or so between thinking and an inner kind of listening, an inner stillness."

So whether you like it or not, just like when a red light forces you to stop your manic driving, a locked-up computer makes you take a break from relentless thought activity. If I can catch myself in time, I take a deep breath and realize how it's my attachment to the importance of what I was doing that is making me suffer over its potential loss.

I don't know how you do a soft boot; I tend to "play" the Ctr-Alt-Del keys all at once like a three-note chord (C-A-D) on a piano. You may arpeggiate them for all I know. The names of the keys are also suggestive. "Control" implies the lack thereof, and that you've reached an impasse. "ALT" suggests that you better try doing something different since all the ranting and pounding you've engaged in up to now has just confirmed your insanity in doing the same thing over and over and expecting different results. "Delete?" Well, that could be a suggestion to take yourself out of the equation, sort of "let go."

The phrase "to boot a computer" is derived from the expression "to lift oneself up by one's bootstraps" which is a physical impossibility, but it implies something being able to go outside of itself. Without asking myself how, I accept the Buddhist teaching that the mind can observe itself acting. ET says something to the effect that being aware that you are unaware is a state of awareness.

So when your overworked computer is smart enough to lock up, it's asking for a "reboot.'

And, when your overworked brain is similarly in need of refreshing, it needs a "re-Buddh-a."

Okay, that "smelled of the lamp." So here's another thought: When a computer freezes or presents a blue screen, there are still signs of life and a hope of recovery.

But when the black screen appears, a soft boot just won't do and you will need to reach down to the power switch and start another session. And some believe that when the black screen of death appears in their lives some power will start the program all over again.

I AM GOING TO DIE
Seiyo Thomas DeMann

My Dharma Glimpse comes from a personal experience where I was given a Second Chance to do it right this time.

Think of your loved ones. Then think of your friends. Think of those involved in this Bright Dawn Lay Ministry Class. Who will be the first in each of these categories to depart from this life? You can't answer this question and if you tried, chances are that you would be wrong. Age has nothing to do with the correct answer. Life is fleeting and we must be ready.

It was July 1, 2002 and as I was leaving the office at the end of the day and wished everyone a goodnight followed by "See you in the morning." Don't make plans. I never saw these fellow employees again. I enjoyed dinner with my wife and left her to attend a social meeting. I stopped at a Barnes & Noble's to get a coffee to take to the meeting and browse through a few books. Suddenly I got a very strange feeling. This feeling persisted so I drove home not remembering how I got there. I went straight to bed. The next two days my wife called in sick for me as I had little recollection of what I was doing. My wife called my physician and he treated me for the flu. On July 4 we watched Independence Day (so states my wife and she tells me I said it was a good movie).....no recollection, whatsoever. We went to bed and that night she remembers me trying to get up during the night time unsuccessfully. The following morning I could not walk.

The next thing I somewhat remember was being in triage at a local hospital. The doctors were puzzled and it took some time for them to diagnose my condition. I had some black dots on my extremities which meant that my system was shutting down. I developed Acute Endocarditis, Cerebrites, and Bacteremia from a staph infection. Every cell in my body was affected. The infection entered my bloodstream, ate away 80% of my heart valve, sending pieces to my brain which caused a stroke. This illness has a survival rate of only 3%. (Since that time I have met nurses in emergency rooms who have never met anyone who survived Acute Endocarditis).

I spent the next 7 weeks in the hospital which included relearning how to walk and function after the stroke. I also had to have open heart surgery to replace the heart valve. I finally did make it to back to work but with a different employer five months later.

I was relatively new to Buddhism but fortunately remembered teachings about impermanence (which I didn't want to address), living in the present moment and fear. Hard to believe but this helped me enjoy this dire time of immobility and helped me to remain in peace and calm. I often think what a valuable and important lesson this experience was for me. How lucky that

Buddhism came into my life shortly before this time especially with the limited knowledge that I had.

What did I learn? Time flies, impermanence does not wait and this body is easily lost! Buddhism, or other practices, are not just a tag that is nice to be a part of. This life is not a game. Do you want to continue on the endless cycle of birth and death or take action? As Buddhists, do you take your practice seriously? The stakes are tremendous. I prefer not to be reborn again (and again and again). I am now on the Pure Land path. Choose your practice and give it your all. Zen, Theravadin, Tibetan, Vipassana ………….. it doesn't matter. Listen to what is taught in your chosen tradition. Try not to get all caught-up in the psychology and intricacies of the practice. Keep it simple. Be serious, be sincere, be honest with yourself.

No one wants to think about death (well, it doesn't bother me any longer) but we must think about it. Why waste your valuable time with idle nonsense? Think about all of the little things we fear and worry about each day. Isn't following the Buddhist path more important than the fears and worries of this life?

We are living in a dream. Wake Up. Do the work. Practice. Be fearless. Do not hide from death, why ignore the inevitable?

I would like to mention a quote from Dr. Arthur Caliandro………."My greatest wisdom has not come through a comfortable existence. It has been achieved during periods of struggle and pain."

Finally, in his book *Living in the Light of Death,* Larry Rosenberg, a Theravada teacher, writes, "when we become intimate with death, we also become profoundly intimate with ourselves, with others and indeed with all things". This was my lesson, and as well, a life-long blessing.

CROCHET
Patti Kayo

For the last few months, I've been learning how to crochet. This is a peaceful, relaxing, portable hobby, and I'm actually getting somewhere with it. There is a practical application: blankets, scarves, and booties for all, and it is also a fact that the world needs more pot holders.

I recently started a slightly advanced scarf project. This scarf has a pattern with a basket-weave effect which involves several twists and turns of the hook and yarn to make a single stitch, so I have to pay close attention.

About 15 inches into my project, which represents about three hours of work, I decided to stop and review what I had done so far. There at the very beginning I noticed a MISTAKE! What? I don't remember doing that. Then I had to decide if I really wanted to undo all my work in order to go back and fix that one wrong stitch. Reminding myself that I'm doing this for fun and relaxation, I decided that leaving in the mistake outweighed the heartache of undoing all the good work. I told myself that it wasn't that noticeable in the grand scheme of things, that I'm still learning, and to just keep going.

And then, oh no, I found another mistake a couple more inches from the beginning! I thought I had been concentrating so hard, one hook and loop at a time. In my mind, I had been "present" the whole time, and I was surprised to see objective evidence that my attention had wandered several times. When I showed the scarf to my husband, Doug, he innocently asked me about a few more areas that looked a little suspicious.

Where was I when I thought I was being so mindful? I wasn't aware of _not_ being aware at any point, but here was the proof. As I thought about it, I remembered -- I had been slightly preoccupied with several concerns: our injured dog, the pain in my neck, what to do with my mother's belongings -- my crocheted scarf had become a timeline of my mental activity. I pointed to the first mistake and told Doug, "This is where I was worrying about our dog, and this is where I was thinking about my neck" and so on.

Although my crocheted scarf shows me when I wasn't "there" for the stitches, how about all the other times in real life when I've just gone through the motions? I don't have a scarf of life to show me that, and I can't unravel what I've done and go back and fix my mistakes in life. But with continued practice I can be more skillful with my crocheting and with living.

By the way, I'm keeping my scarf with all its imperfections as a reminder to stay focused in the present.

PERSPECTIVE
Andy Goyo Bondy

The constant interplay between what is real -- what is 'out there' and how we behave towards those things -- what we 'see,' 'hear' or whatever -- is in constant flux. The moment you are sure that what you 'see' is real, then you've forgotten that seeing is something you do. The Buddha knew this distinction clearly. Pointing to the moon is not the same as the moon. Or, "There is hearing...I hear through my ears...I perceive the things I hear through my ears."

What brought me back to this relationship is an odd experience I am periodically having, something I first noticed last week. I was sitting in my car and while I opened the door, a green LCD light came on my dashboard. I happened to be focusing on the steering wheel so the image of the light stereoscopically split in two -- but while seeing two lights did not surprise me, I realized one was green and one was blue! So I began to alternate which eye was open and recognized that my left eye reported the light was green but my right eye reported it was blue -- not blue-green but clearly a blue. I repeated this experiment with other similar lights in the house -- on the microwave for example. When I stared at the light with both eyes open I saw green but if I continued to stare I could detect the faint blue that was being suppressed by the more dominant green.

Now you might reasonably ask, which eye saw the world as it is -- and you might say 'the one seeing green' -- but that would depend upon other people identifying that tint as 'green.' There is no independent way of determining which eye was correct. And of course they both could be wrong! Now, some would talk about the information that the brain was processing and then talk about what the brain saw -- but this leads to endless trouble. The brain does nothing, the eyes do nothing -- the entire person acts. (Rest assured, I saw my ophthalmologist today and he saw something funky about my retina so I get to see another specialist next week!)

For me, this experience is the type that challenges our long held belief that "I" know what the world is actually like -- my perspective, my perception is the true one and others simply fail to see the world the proper way -- my way. This points out the multiple sources of influence upon our behavior and that often we cannot describe at all why we are doing what we are doing.

This issue of 'perspective' involves other actions that reflect our perceptual biases. In graduate school, one professor told of some work he did with a woman who was extremely obese. She was so overweight that he realized that he could not possibly get her to change all aspects of her eating. So he aimed to tackle just one meal- breakfast. He started by asking what she typically ate for breakfast. She told him she usually ate a dozen biscuits, 6 eggs, 6 slices of bacon, and several cups of juice and coffee. He thought that if she could cut down on just the biscuits, things must improve. So he asked if she thought she could eat just one biscuit while not changing anything else about her breakfast. She said 'yes!' Over the next several weeks he monitored that she lost no weight whatsoever. She insisted that she did exactly what he asked- ate one biscuit and did not change anything else about her eating patterns all day long. After about a month of no improvement, he called the woman's husband to check on whether she was telling the truth. Her husband replied, "Yes indeed, doc -- she eats just one biscuit in the morning. She takes the same amount of dough she used to make a dozen biscuits and now makes just one!"

How many times a day do we fool ourselves about the 'new me' and my 'new behaviors?' How many times do I report what I see as if it were reality as it is, unfettered by all the contingencies that influence my actions? In reading about Right Thinking, it becomes clear that there is no Right Thinking in isolation. Unless I continuously check on how my perceptions relate to the reported perceptions of those around me, I can have no confidence on either what I am perceiving or what I am reporting (even to myself) about what I am perceiving.

For me at this moment, there are aspects of the environment to which if asked, "Is it green or is it blue?" I must honestly answer "Yes!"

Now go eat some biscuits... or maybe just one...

THE POWER OF THEN
Douglas Kuyo Slaten

Coming up in our readings for the Bright Dawn Lay Ministry group is a book by Eckhart Tolle called *The Power of Now*. Just by the title it's clear that he's going to be talking about mindfulness and the importance of "being in the moment," to use the popular phrase.

But I'd like to talk about the power of "Then."

What or where is "Then?" "Then" is anywhere but the here and now, it is the opposite of "Suchness," and is the place where I spend most of my waking hours. It is a continuing dream that things were either better in the past or will be in the future. In fact, if I practice any kind of Buddhism, it would probably be called "Then Buddhism."

What is the power of "Then?" The power of "Then" is its ability to make us spend our lives chasing an endlessly receding landscape trying to get to a place where we eventually hope to rest. But in fact, we don't really want to get to that point. Because being still means having to face the truth of impermanence, so we fill our minds with more distractions to put off that moment of truth indefinitely.

Where does the power of "Then" come from? Buddhism tells us that it comes from ourselves, from our ego-driven need to complicate the world and establish a place for ourselves in it. The power of "Then" is manifested by our incessant need for variety and distraction in our lives or what Rev. Dr. Nobuo Haneda calls "augmenting and decorating our existence from outside." In the daily round of life "Then" generates the feeling that we are getting behind, so we try to accumulate extra time by working harder and multi-tasking.

The Dutch author, Janwillem van de Wetering, tells a story from the year he spent in a Zen monastery in Japan. On one occasion he was scolded for his lack of concentration and mindfulness. The Master or Head Monk who had seen him urinating and brushing his teeth at the same time yelled, "you are making a mess of the toilet and your mouth!" I think it's interesting that even there, in an environment specially designed to be conducive to living in the "Now," it was necessary for him to distract himself with compulsive behavior.

Computers, cell phones and other technological marvels actually make work and keep us busier. Which is the point. Their real functions are as distractions from the familiar, the ordinary, the real. To paraphrase Jack Nicholson, in the movie *A Few Good Men,* "we can't handle the truth." So the trend in the world is to view reality through any number of electronic enhancements. Nature is more vivid when seen on a big screen plasma TV. People are more interesting when called on a cell phone, texted, or visited on Facebook, rather than met in person. To sum it up, virtual reality is becoming preferable to "real" reality.

At this point in my rant I find myself thinking that this isn't really much of an insight. It's really just another observation on our gloomy conditional existence. More of a Dharma "gloompse" than "Glimpse." But this is my path. I've come to terms with the fact that I'm unlikely to have the "burning bush" type of spiritual awakening but will make whatever progress I can through hard work and introspection. But from what I've heard, the gate is wide and that is the way others have taken.

So how can I get from "Then" to "Now"? In his eight-point program for spiritual living, Eknath Easwaran offers this deceptively simple advice: "slow down." More specifically, this includes:

1 Give yourself more time
2 Don't crowd your day
3 Ask what's important
4 Take time for relationships
5 Take time for reflection
6 Don't let yourself get hurried
7 Cultivate patience
8 Slow down your mind

Some of these I have been practicing for some time. Some need more work. The last, "slow down your mind," is almost impossible for me to do; when I start the day with a morning meditation I must first ignore my mind, which is screaming at me to turn on the computer and get busy before I get further behind. But I know this is an illusion and that, if I am still, the demands of "Then" will eventually become quieter.

"Then" = hurrying, multi-tasking, distraction, confusion, noise

"Now" = slowing down, single-pointed attention, mindfulness, peace, silence.

SIMPLICITY
Seiyo Thomas DeMann

I was re-reading one of my favorite Pure Land books, *Taming the Monkey Mind*, and a commentary by the author stopped me cold in my tracks. The author wrote that *The sage Confucious once said: "Eating leftover rice, drinking rainwater, with my arms as a head-rest, I still feel happy inside. Such is the happiness of the wise"*.

This forced me to ask the question of why do we spend so much time accumulating things? It may be because of the prompting of our ego. Accumulating leads to less free time because there is often maintenance involved when acquiring odds and ends. In the *Tao Te Ching* Lao Tzu talked about the importance of simplicity (Ch. 67). He said that if one is simple in actions and thoughts, you return to the source of being.

In his One-Page Testament, Honen Shonin, the founder of Jodo Shu, was talking about the practice of Nembutsu. He instructed everyone to forget about practicing like scholars who studied and understood the deep meaning of this mantra and to behave like simple-minded folks, who know not a single letter, or like ignorant nuns or monks, whose faith is implicitly simple.

Finally, in the introduction of *Everyday Suchness* William Gilbert writes "The greatest truths have always been the most simple".

What is the importance of simplicity, I asked myself? Fortunately, in my situation I have not accumulated many things in my lifetime and that works out just fine with me. I then don't worry about losing my possessions. I don't have a management position in my work so I don't have to worry about my managerial performance in upper management's opinion. I don't have a fancy car so I don't worry about minor scratches and dings. I don't worry about climbing up the corporate ladder where there is back-stabbing. How great this is. With all of this in mind, life is pretty good.

What would have happened if I had fame and fortune? I don't believe that I would then be on the most important spiritual journey that I am on. I would probably be reaching and grasping for what I thought would bring me happiness. My peace of mind and security would not exist. I am glad and fortunate to live simply. I do have a pillow and drink water from a Brita filter and appreciate these little things immensely. I can appreciate a meal at McDonald's since I don't need to impress anyone. For entertainment I can enjoy staring at the mountains. (All I now need is to get the *wise* part perfected that Confucius referred to).

Simplicity in life is good. I can be happy if I choose to be!

EXPECT THE UNEXPECTED
Douglas Kuyo Slaten

Setup:
For the past few days I've been annoyed over being handed a work assignment that's going to require me to give a PowerPoint presentation. I feel that this is really someone else's responsibility but that it is typical that I would get stuck with this "Dirty Harry" type of job that no one else will take.

Discussion:
I don't like giving live presentations. Okay, okay, I have a fear of public speaking. It's not crippling but I certainly don't look forward to doing it. When I am forced to give a presentation, I experience a lot of anxiety and waste a great deal of time worrying about how it's going to go. I often over-prepare hoping that I will be letter-perfect and "bullet-proof" even though I know that during the Q&A I can expect to be thrown a "zinger" by the smartest person in the audience. Given the nature of my job these speaking occasions are going to arise from time to time, yet, since I never know the exact moment the unexpected will strike, I have the same initial reactions of irritation/anger and worry/fear. Eventually, of course, I accept my situation and go on to do the job at hand but only after working through the same painful process.

Dharma-analysis:
What's really going on here? Let's see, the First Noble Truth says that I am going to experience dukkha no matter what. And, although for some people public speaking isn't a big deal, and for others it may even be enjoyable, to me it's dukkha.

The Second Noble Truth says that the cause of my dukkha is attachment. Where, how, to what? Well, judging by my initial negative reaction I seem to be attached to the idea that I can, with careful, meticulous planning, control the timing of these unpleasant events, prepare accordingly, and thereby avoid or at least minimize the unpleasantness. The fact that this approach has never worked very well for me in the past has not been a deterrent to continuing to use it. I guess another option would be to quit my job, throw away my phone and never answer the door. Interestingly, I have a brother who pretty much lives like this. Predictably, he still gets his share of dukkha, too.

The above two responses remind me of the extremes of asceticism and hedonism which the Buddha warns us to avoid. Taking the excessive worry and over-preparation path is like ascetic self-mortification, and trying to avoid all responsibility is extreme selfishness. So what's the middle way in this case?

The Glimpse:

A corollary of the First Noble Truth is that human existence is marked by impermanence. If at the moment I am in the happy state of not doing public speaking, I can expect that there will come a time when that's what I will be doing. Then that too will pass. So instead of trying to interfere with this law I should work within it. When something comes up that needs to be done I don't need to predict the outcome or hang on to the results after it's over. I accept responsibility, do it as well as I can (remembering "good enough is good enough") and then let it go.

All this time I've been talking about how to address a limited and to some a rather trivial problem, but the approach is the same when dealing with the most serious issues life can offer, and presupposes acquiring those qualities of humor, spontaneity, flexibility and adaptability that we associate with the person who is fully aware and living in the present moment. I should live so long!

STRESS
Seiyo Thomas DeMann

I wrote this glimpse shortly after I became aware that it would soon be my turn to share a Dharma Glimpse with the class. Soon after I wrote this we lost Bubba, but I will always think of the many teachings that I learned from him. Therefore, I chose to share this glimpse today in his memory.

There are two great teachers that I constantly learn from in my household. I am a humble disciple of my wife, Lynn, and our greyhound, Bubba. "Bubba" is what he was called by his trainer at the racetrack. His real name is "Deep in Thought" (what a great Buddhist name). If you were able to spend some time with Bubba you would see that his real name is very appropriate. Recently a Dharma Glimpse was given to me by Bubba. Bubba shared a teaching with me that Shakyamuni Buddha gave us in the first chapter of the Dhammapada when he said: "Our life is shaped by our mind; we become what we think."

Stress is the way that one responds to a situation. It is normally solved by either "fight" or "flight."

In late September of this year, it was time to get our carpets cleaned. Usually we have four rooms done. My wife decided that this time we would have all six rooms done. It sounded easy enough. We would stay in our uncarpeted kitchen with the dog until the carpets dried. The kitchen is in the center of the house and a half wall encloses it from the rest of the house. There is a nice big window in the room and we are able to get much light from the surrounding rooms. What I am trying to say is that the kitchen is very "open." We used a TV table and a folding chair to keep Bubba from escaping to the carpets where he spends all of his time. Easier said than done, and he somehow snuck out of the room and we had to retrieve him. It was amazing to see a tall 70-pound dog "sneak out." Bubba is terrified of things like tile floors, stairways and closets.

What we figured out is that he was out of his comfort zone, even though he was in a spacious area and with us. He became very restless and it was apparent that he was in stress mode. Before the carpets dried, I left for a massage and my wife took Bubba for a walk in the park. While I was still gone she arrived back at the house but found that the carpets were not quite ready to be walked on. So it was back to the kitchen for a bit. Bubba could not take the so-called confinement any longer and began to hyperventilate. My wife had to cover him with wet towels and washcloths to cool him off. He worked himself into quite a frenzy; he could have easily died without proper attention.

"Our life is shaped by our mind; we become what we think." I cannot imagine what was going through the dog's mind. He became so stressed and fearful of what? It did not matter. Since he was not in his normal routine, that was enough to terrorize him.

How often do we do something as irrational as this? The answer for me is many times. Our minds tell us that something is not right, not normal and fear sets in. Fear of the bad things that will happen to us now (but rarely do). There is a slogan that says most of the things we worry about will never happen.

"Our life is shaped by our mind; we become what we think." Worry and fear are two very useless emotions. Why not think of happiness, gratitude, helping others, good deeds, giving, etc.? The First Noble Truth speaks of suffering. The Dhammapada explains it well "Our life is shaped by our mind; we become what we think."

We have already adopted our new greyhound, Happy. He is already teaching me lessons!

GOLDEN AND SILVER RULES
Douglas Kuyo Slaten

The idea for this dharma glimpse came to me as I was driving to work, a time when my mind tends to wander freely. I had just done something uncivil, like preventing someone from getting in front of me. Of course, I had some sort of justification why they shouldn't get ahead of me in "my" lane, and although at these times I have the uncomfortable feeling that I'm doing something wrong, it's overruled by the desire not to let the other car violate my "rights." Then it occurred to me to consider putting my rationalizations aside and just ask myself how I would feel if what I had just done to that person had been done to me.

My thought, which goes in and out of focus, is the practical distinction between the positive version of the "Golden Rule" ("<u>Do</u> unto others, etc.") and its negative expression ("<u>Don't do</u>...") which is sometimes called the "Silver Rule." A quick Google search supplied the following list, and I was surprised to see how many times it was the "silver" version that appeared:

Brahmanism: this is the sum of duty: Do naught unto others which would cause you pain if done to you. (Mahabharata 5:1517)

Buddhism: Hurt not others in ways that you yourself would find hurtful. (UdanaVarga 5:18)

Christianity: All things whatsoever ye would that man should do to you, do ye even so to them; for this is the law and the prophets. (Matthew 7:12)

Confucianism: Surely it is the maxim of loving-kindness: Do not do unto others what you would not have them do unto you. (Analects 15:23)

Islam: No one of you is a believer until he desires for his brother that which he desires for himself. (Sunnah)

Judaism: What is hateful to you, do not to your fellowman. That is the entire law; all the rest is commentary. (Talmud, Shabbat 31a)

Taoism: Regard your neighbor's gain as your own gain and your neighbor's loss as your own loss. (T'ai Shang Kan Ying P'ien)

Zoroastrianism: That nature alone is good which refrains from doing unto another whatsoever is not good for itself. (Dadistan-I-dinik 94:5)

These positive and negative ways of expressing this ethic brings to mind the Bodhisattva/Arhat ideals. The Bodhisattva, who aspires for all beings to be enlightened, is a "do-gooder" and represents the positive, active expression of the rule, while the Arhat is pictured as being concerned with personal enlightenment and with the negative goal of "just" not doing harm. So the "golden" version found in Christian scriptures, to our Western ears sounds more robust, more positive.

Speaking for myself, I find it fairly easy most of the time to perform little acts of charity and kindness as a matter of course. And particularly when I'm feeling good and things are going my way, good deeds come easily and just make me feel even better. But it's when the *shenpa* is rising and I'm feeling abused, that it's hard to remember that the other person can't know what I'm feeling and to say to myself, "Don't do that since you wouldn't want that done to you."

For example, suppose when you are angry or annoyed for what seems like a good reason you become withdrawn and sullen. This behavior can be justified in your own mind, but the people around you don't always have access to that information. All they know is that your behavior is making them unhappy. And according to the "Silver Rule," that's all you need to know not to act that way.

Practicing the "Silver Rule" is hard since it is basically a type of prevention. By not doing a certain thing, you are preventing an undesirable situation from arising. The guiding principle of medicine is found in the Latin phrase "primum non nocere," which means, "first do no harm," and as a public health physician I know that prevention is always preferable to treatment. But there's not much glory in preventive medicine since when prevention works, nothing happens! If you want recognition, go into surgery. In the same way, even if you are trying to be humble, good actions tend to be appreciated and acknowledged, while people are rarely conscious of the times when you restrained yourself from behaving badly.

So the point I'm trying to make, and it's going to take forever at this rate, is that even though the two versions of the rule appear to amount to the same thing, they are not. When you practice the "Golden Rule," you are visibly doing the right thing. What's hard is not to do the wrong thing even though no one will reward you simply because it's the way you would like to be treated.

GRATITUDE
Seiyo Thomas DeMann

Gratitude has always been a shortcoming of mine. Recently, however, this has begun to change slowly. With this in mind, I have started to have thoughts of things that I need to be grateful for as I travel on my current path.

Shakyamuni Buddha tells a story of how lucky one is to be born a human. Gautama says that being born a human is as difficult as if a blind turtle rises to the top of the ocean once every hundred years and his head slips into a yoke as he reaches the top, improbable but not impossible. How fortunate am I! Because I was born a human, I have the ability to hear and accept the Dharma which can lead me to enlightenment and nirvana. I would not have this opportunity if I were born an animal.

Previously, I wrote a Dharma Glimpse regarding the illness that nearly took my life. It was at this point that things started to change for me in my way of thinking. Exactly what is this life all about? From what I have learned in one of the books that we read in this class by Kogen Mizuno who made the statement, "What is the final profound truth? *It is the finding of the infinite life of humankind within the eternal life-force of the universe.*" I found this to be a comforting statement and something to work at. So how do I work at this? So what am I grateful for?

First of all, I am grateful for my illness even though I am left with various physical and psychological limitations. This encouraged my walk down the Buddhist path to find something. Siddhartha Gautama has pointed his finger to show me what I need to do.

I have learned that life is composed of suffering. If I do not understand this, I will not search for a way to eliminate this suffering.

From this.........I have learned the following:

I have learned that I should see things as they are. If I am unable to do this, this will lead to nothing but misunderstanding and delusion.

I have learned that every cause has an effect. If I do not realize this, my actions will create ill effects. I must control every thought, action and how I speak. These three things make up my actions.

I have learned the Four Noble Truths are a way to lead me to enlightenment and nirvana. If I do not understand this, I will be lost in this lifetime.

I have learned that the Eightfold Path is THE way to escape this misery. If I do not understand this, I will have a miserable existence.

I have learned that the Six Paramitas are also a way to escape to the other shore. If I do not understand this, I will miss the opportunity to have taken a short walk in this lifetime on the Bodhisattva path and not been able to help others if even the smallest way.

I have learned the importance of belonging to a Sangha such as this one. If I do not understand this, I would not have come to all of these realizations.

I have learned the importance and significance of this class. If I do not understand this, I would not appreciate the two leaders of this class and how each class member has added to my spiritual growth.

Perhaps gratitude is no longer a shortcoming of mine. With that in mind.................Thank you Rev. Kubose, Adrienne-san and to all my classmates. I am going to be okay.

These are only my spiritual benefits. I have not even mentioned family, friends, employment, food, shelter and clothing. However, only what I have absorbed in my spiritual experience is what I can take with me. I will eventually be separated from everything else.

Thank you Shakyamuni, for pointing your finger to show me the way.

Bright Dawn Dharma Glimpses:

LAY MINISTER CLASS #5

EVERY DAY IS A GOOD DAY.
Linda Shoyo Wisniewski

I had an experience about a month ago which showed me in a very concrete way that when I am in the present moment, in the NOW moment, nothing is happening and I am in a state of just beingness - it is very peaceful.

However, if I'm not peaceful, what is the problem?

Is something or someone out there disturbing my peace of mind? Is it the hot humid weather we get in the Midwest taking away my ability to have a good day? Does an argument with a loved one ruin my day? Can anything in my life ruin my decision to have a good day?

I'm learning that nothing can ruin my decision to have a good day except my thoughts. Here are several examples of this.

My husband has been sober for more than 25 years. He recently spent 10 days in Italy and enjoyed tasting their wines and aperitifs. When he came home, we went out to a Greek restaurant for dinner and he ordered a beer. I started to panic, although I didn't say anything to him. But the thoughts in my mind were saying a lot. The thoughts were trying to scare me and make me believe that now my husband was going to turn into an alcoholic again; what would I do if that happened; I don't want to live with an alcoholic; the voices in my mind went on and on.

In reality, nothing was really happening except the loud thoughts in my mind were robbing me of the peace and joy I had been experiencing at the restaurant with my family.

The fact is: My family and I were having dinner, we were all drinking a beer, and I wasn't upset with anyone else drinking a beer - only with my husband based on past history. The disturbance was caused by my thoughts that were bringing the past into the present moment.

Another example that demonstrates how our thoughts and beliefs cause all of our disturbances is when I imagine a situation that hasn't even happened yet. For example, I'm planning a visit with family and the visit hasn't even happened but I remember that in the past visits, we would always argue about some stupid thing. All of a sudden I found myself having imaginary conversations in my mind about how I would defend myself if I was judged or criticized. I found I was getting angry just thinking about the possibility and yet nothing was going on in the moment; it was all being played out in my mind.

So what I have been learning is that no circumstance or person can rob me of my peace. Nothing outside my mind can really hurt me or upset me in any way. It's only my thoughts about something from the past or an imagined future that can disturb my peace.

Now, when I find myself getting riled up, fearful, worried or anxious I start asking myself, "Linda, right now, what is happening?" Then I start to laugh because I realize nothing is happening except my "stinking" thinking and my Fantasies.

In the NOW, I can be at peace in every moment. It's a decision I could make. Every moment can be a peaceful one; every day is a good day.

DHARMA RAIN
Mark Kaiyo Fives

At my job, rain halts our work and creates a welcomed break. We all congregate in a maintenance building until it passes, or in cases where it looks like it will stick around for a while, we are sent home.

Last week, while sitting at work watching the rain fall, I found myself lost in contemplation, and I discovered that rain is a perfect model to inspire us in our Buddhist lives. A model that contains many teachings to be discovered.

If we look at the life of a single raindrop, we can see that it leads a very enlightened existence.

Born in the clouds, a raindrop begins its short life as a drop falling to the earth, with no aspirations to be anything more than a raindrop. Not dwelling in the past or worrying about the future, just being the best raindrop that it can be in the here and now.

At the end of its short life, it reaches the earth. With no regrets, it gladly falls exactly where it is supposed to be, having lived in harmony with the universe. Maybe it will be absorbed into the earth, a river, or an ocean, where it begins a new life. Maybe it will be absorbed into the roots of a tree. What once was a tiny raindrop, now becomes part of a mighty tree. Maybe it will drop into a lazy stream, to be sipped by a newborn fawn. Maybe it will just land on a sidewalk, waiting on the sun's evaporating heat to take it back to the clouds where it can become a raindrop once again.

In this way, the tiny raindrop teaches us about transmigration, or rebirth and death, as well as the naturalness of all life.

WINE
Roger Seiyo Cochran

This last weekend we had supper with friends. Ray left a book with me, saying that it reminded him of Buddhism and he thought I would be interested. I looked at the title, <u>Reading Between the Wines</u>, and then put it aside.

When I began reading the book it was quite a surprise to me, a genuine Dharma Glimpse as seen from the point of view of wines.

> *"A wine is complex when it suggests something that can't be seen or even known, but it is definitely, and hauntingly, there. A complex wine seems to channel the very complexity of living. A complicated wine is just a mosaic we piece together with our senses. Here's what I think you're after: a point of utter receptivity in which you're seeing only the wine instead of seeing yourself seeing the wine." (p. 20).*

I read this, and other descriptions:

> *" ...wine will contrive to confuse your assumptions in order to force you to still your ego and listen....Remember, your palate isn't a thing you possess; it is part of you. You don't taste with this thing: you taste with your whole self" (p. 21).*

> *"I am immersed in the world, the world is immersed in me. There are filaments and connections, always buzzing and always alive. The world is not a commodity designed for my use: its cells are my cells, its secrets are my secrets. And every once in a while, usually when I least expect it, wine draws it's mouth to my ear and says things to me. 'Time is not what you think. A universe can live inside a speck of flavor. There are doors everywhere to millions of interlocking worlds. Beauty is always closer than it seems...'" (p. 27-28).*

This struck me so powerfully that I felt the presence of the Dharma. I knew I had read this before and had to pull an old book out. This is what Dogen Zenji was saying (I think) in "The Time-Being" when he said, "Each moment is all being, it is the entire world. Reflect now whether any being or any world is left out of the present moment." (p. 77. <u>Moon in a Dewdrop</u>. Trans K. Tanahashi. 1985, original about 1239 AD).

The Dharma is everywhere, even where least expected: with a friend who translates sutras without knowing their source; in a bottle of Malbec.

EVERYTHING IS A DHARMA GLIMPSE
David Kakuyo Wisniewski

I am having a hard time coming up with a Glimpse and I don't know why. I have talked to Linda about my ideas and she could not see any connection to the idea of Dharma. But I see them and I did not understand why I am unable to convey them clearly. Today it came to me that what I was saying really did not make sense because I had not made a connection.

Everything I do, hear or say is a Dharma Glimpse.

Simple (maybe) as this statement sounds, it was like a very big bomb going off in my mind. The few books we have read and talked about were in my subconscious and swirling around and around. I was making connections and didn't realize it. I could not put these thoughts into meaningful words and I am still having a hard time. Not every Dharma Glimpse is an "AHA MOMENT". I was looking for a point in time, an action in time, something to hang my hat onto, something to wrap around the concept of Dharma. Dharma is life. My morning greeting is not social grease, a meaningless group of words. It has turned into a greeting on a deeper level (for me) of: I see you, I hear you, we are here together.

Everything I do, hear or say is a Dharma Glimpse.

Last week I had a phone conversation with a son-in-law. This man is not my favorite person in this world. Not who he is, but his actions toward my stepdaughter and her child. I know this is a judgment, and I am not comfortable in my thoughts about him. Well, he called in a great panic and fear. I had, in the past, been under the power of alcohol, and he needed my help. My last drink was over 24 years ago, and after many AA meetings and much soul searching I know the power that drives people to drink. I listened and heard his words. I gave no comfort or excuses. I told him what I had to do to save myself and that he must drive to a meeting and open the door to say the words "I am an alcoholic". He did not want to hear this and tried to wiggle around to get free. Sometimes in life we must face our fears and we must face them by ourselves to show ourselves that courage, as well as fear, is inside us. The next step is his choice. After the call (it lasted over two hours) I felt a strange peace. The call was about acceptance and a reaching out. Have my feelings towards him changed? Yes and No. I hope he finds the man inside himself that does not shame him.

Everything I do, hear or say is a Dharma Glimpse.

This Monday Linda and I went to a water park in Wisconsin Dells and spent the day with our daughters and grandchildren GETTING WET. What fun it is to be under the spell of small children. What amazement it is to look though the eyes of joy.

Everything I do, hear or say is a Dharma Glimpse.

Talking like this is very foreign to me and I feel that I must hide the new thoughts, even from myself. I think that others will judge that what I say is false. I see now that I have hidden who and what I am for a very long time. The Dharma, the Way, the Buddha, the Four Noble Truths have given me the wisdom to let it hang out there... to realize that who or what I am has to come from within and that I want to be a man that I am not ashamed of.

Everything I do, hear or say is a Dharma Glimpse.

BLAME
Tamu Hoyo Ngina

Something happened about a week ago. Rev. Koyo Sensei sent out an email from *DailyOM*. The title of the email was "Blaming Others," so I clicked it to see what it was about. The subject of this *DailyOM* was listed under "Burdensome Feelings" and was written by Madisyn Taylor. The title in big bold letters was:

"We cannot insist that someone take responsibility for their actions; only they can make the choice when they are ready."

I have to be honest and say that this is something that I struggle with a great deal. That day that Reverend Koyo had forwarded that email to everyone, it was like a "boom," it was right there, it was exactly what I needed to see and read in that moment and to sort of simmer down.

Because actually, that day I was having a bit of a problem with someone in my life. You know when you love someone very deeply and you have known them for a very long time, there will always be these issues. We all have our various issues that crop up, our lessons we need to learn, our habits or what have you, and sometimes they affect other people's lives. Sometimes they continue to affect our own lives, yet we are not quite able to get over them.

So it was an issue I was having with someone. It was like I was just feeling, and I was wishing "Wow, I just wish this person would take responsibility for their actions." And the more I wished that and the more I went deeper into that feeling, the more I began to suffer. And by "suffer" I mean really be stressed out, really be upset, really, in that timeframe, start to color not necessarily the feelings that I had for that person but my interaction with that person. I would feel stressed and agitated every time I spoke to that person.

And then this email came and it was like a Mack truck right in my face. And it really gave me something to think about. And of course I then felt the need to really vent and get certain feelings out. The more I read the big bold title **"We cannot insist someone take responsibility for their actions; only they can make that choice when they are ready,"** I saw in that a lesson for myself as well.

I have to take responsibility for MY actions and for my reactions to another person. As much as I might feel the suffering feeling from wanting the other person to stand up and take responsibility and change their life, it wasn't doing anything for that other person. It was helping me to suffer, and it was helping my relationship with that other person to suffer.

Then I realized that, wait a minute, the second part of that title, "Only they can make the choice when they are ready"... I had to realize that only I could make the choice for myself when I was ready, that I was no longer to allow the actions of this other person, whom I love very much, to affect me in such a way that I chose to react and put myself into a situation of suffering, nor put the other person into a situation of suffering because I was unhappy with their actions or lack of responsibility for their actions. I had to step back a moment and accept responsibility for the thoughts that were in my head, for the need to continue to think that this person needed to change.

Also, I started to realize that I had no right to insist that this person change or needed to form their life on a path that I thought was best for them. No matter how much I thought I loved them, they have their own life and their own path to take. Even if they took a path that seemed unhelpful or unhealthy for them, I needed to make the choice.

On that day, after much thought, after much back and forth and much venting, I had to make a choice to let it go. Once I began to do that, to make the choice to let go, it was sort of like my energy shifted.

I do the updates for Bright Dawn Center of Buddhism's Facebook page. I always like to mix it up a little bit. I like to use quotes from Rev. Gyomay's and Rev. Koyo's writings, from various different Dharma teachers, and various sects of Buddhism.

That day, after I resolved the letting-go issue, I took down Reverend Koyo's book *Bright Dawn: Discovering Your Everyday Spirituality*. The very page that I opened up to had this wonderful paragraph in it. The quote was so apropos that I decided to use it. It was as follows:

"In our interpersonal interactions, some things are worth remembering while other things are best forgotten. Wisdom is knowing the difference. In a sense, wisdom is having a selective poor memory. In one of the Buddhist Sutras it is said:

'Some people are like letters carved in rock; they are easily angered and they keep their angry thoughts for a long time. Some people are like letters written in sand; they give way to anger also, but the angry thoughts quickly pass away. Some people are like letters written on water; they let verbal abuse pass them by and no disturbing thoughts are retained.'"

Rev. Koyo's book is one of my favorite Dharma books to read from time to time. AND as I read that and as the words popped out to me…"wisdom"…"rock"…"anger"… the images of letters written in the sand came to me. How many of us have gone to the beach and written our name in the sand or hearts in the sand only to have the waves come wash it away almost immediately. Sometimes we might have a contest with the ocean to see how quickly we can write or rewrite in the sand before the waves can come wash away our words.

This quote from the Buddhist Sutra really stuck to me. You know, I want to blossom into wisdom. I realize wisdom does not come with age. I believe wisdom comes through our experiences and our ability to learn from those experiences and truly take to heart what we have learned and that those experiences, those feelings we have about them and the knowledge we gain from them become a part of our core. That is a part of how I think wisdom develops.

I have been that person who has written letters in the rock. I have been the person whose letters are written in the sand. And every once in a while if I am really lucky, I have also been that person whose letters are written on the water.

When I read those lines it was like a message written to me, and I know it's a message for a lot of people -- that sometimes there are people that you love or people that you interact with in life that may rub you the wrong way, and it's like you just have to let those interactions go, and you have to keep going.

That is the message and Dharma Glimpse that I wanted to share with you. And when I look back at **"We cannot insist that someone take responsibility for their actions, only they can make the choice when they are ready,"** I can just say to myself, "I have to take responsibility for my actions, my reactions, as well as my interactions." And I have to make that choice for myself (when I am ready) and so does everyone else around me (when they are ready).

Thank you very much for allowing me to share my Dharma Glimpse with you and giving you a little peek into my world and my monkey-mind-crazy thoughts!

Thank you, everyone. Gassho. Until next time…

DAUGHTER'S WEDDING
Dorothy Shinyo Merrick

My daughter is getting married May 4, 2013. Besides contributing financially to her event, I am sewing her veil. The idea came from a girlfriend of mine who did this for her daughter. Although I am not a seamstress, she assured me I could do this. In essence, it's hand-beading a gazillion beads in a slippery fabric! (My girlfriend said it was easy for her because she enjoyed sewing, and it was relaxing.) It sounded good—I decided I'll give it a try!

So last fall I purchased the veil material (a light-weight web fabric), beads (all different sizes) thread, needles, etc. I took it home and proceeded to cut the design, but something did not seem right: Yes, my cut was not done correctly, so back to the store for more fabric, and try again! The second time it was right!

Okay, now comes the tedious part—every single bead had to be hand-sewn around the edge of the fabric. The design of the beads included three different shapes and sizes. The key is to knot every few beads so they stay attached with movement once the veil is complete and being worn. I did *not* find this fun or relaxing like my girlfriend did—it was tedious work.

I finished this part at Christmas.

In January, it was time to attach the veil material to the head comb. After careful planning, that was completed. The finishing component was to bead the top of the comb. This is on my "to do" list for today and I'm sure I'll get it done. Yeah!!

I feel proud that I gave my daughter part of me for many months leading up to the wedding. This was time she did not know we spent together, but she was in my heart and in my head (especially once when a needle slipped into my finger tip). It was because of love that I completed this veil.

Her dress fitting (with veil) is next week. She knows I am bringing it, and I can't wait to see her in it! It will be a moment to remember.

So, for me, this veil is a teaching of Buddhism—about our connectedness and our unlimited capacity to give. That said, I'm still glad I have only one daughter!

DHARMA EYES
Mark Kaiyo Fives

I've worked outside for many years. Now, as I look back on those years, I remember the work that was at hand, but not much of anything else. It's as if I was looking at the world through eyes covered with a film of dust.

Five years ago, or maybe more, I became a seeker on a spiritual path—a path that led me to discover the teachings of the Buddha. The voices of the teachers that I've met along the way have been like a Dharma breeze that's blown away some of that dust.

Now I'm beginning to see the world in a much different way. Maybe it's being mindful, or more aware, of what's going on around me; it's an awakening.

Now I see a world of wonder and beauty that lies before me. I'm surrounded by ponds of blue water; by tall, majestic pines, and rainbows of foliage that blanket the landscape; by the gliding of birds that fly high in the sky; by rabbits that hop on by.

I've come to realize the beauty of nature and my oneness with it. This world is truly a paradise of sights, smells and sounds. With every new moment, there are discoveries to be found.

Now, while working, rather than letting it all pass me by, I find myself pausing to take in the beauty of this world.

> *For so many years, I've had partial sight,*
> *I've lived my life without any light.*
>
> *The teachers I've met, the Dharma breeze blew,*
> *Now I see light and am living anew.*
>
> *Before life was bland,*
> *But now it is grand.*
>
> *The Dharma breeze blew,*
> *And life is anew.*
>
> *This world is a wonder of sights, smells and sounds,*
> *With every new moment, discoveries to be found.*
>
> *Make it your cause,*
> *And take time to pause.*
>
> *Enjoying this life*
> *Without any strife.*

SCRUBBING THE FLOOR
– HARMONIZING THE MIND
Linda Shoyo Wisniewski

Housekeeping and doing chores is not something I like doing, and it's especially stressful when company is coming.

I guess it goes back to when I was growing up and I wasn't expected to do chores. Every week we had someone come in and clean the house, and when something needed to be fixed, we hired someone. There was a great dichotomy in thinking and judging those that used their intellect as opposed to those that used their hands. I grew up with an arrogance that housework was "beneath me."

When I was a single parent, I only did what was absolutely necessary and spent most of my time outside doing what I considered important work or having fun with the kids.

But, I like to have people over and then cleaning up becomes a very stressful task. I am learning from my studies that I did so much for "show." I also put so much stress on my husband to make the house look perfect so I can believe that others would believe I was "perfect."

So, I was really surprised when I decided to invite 10 people over for a Hanukkah party. I observed for the first time that I wasn't having this party to impress anyone but the motivation for it was coming from a deep inner joy that was bubbling up in me. This sense of joy informed all my actions.

The day before the party, I got down on my hands and knees and scrubbed each separate tile in the linoleum. As I was scrubbing, I remembered what Rev. Koyo Sensei said at one of our meetings: "You don't have to conquer a stressful task; you can harmonize with it." In the moments I was on my hands and knees, I felt in harmony with the action of scrubbing down all the residue of dirt and grease that had accumulated. It was as if my mind was also being scrubbed of all judgments and resentments.

I was totally in the Now moment and felt so energized. I wasn't conflicted about doing something based on "should," but my thoughts and actions were in harmony and it was joyful.

I also felt as I was on my knees that I was bowing in gratitude to the three treasures of Buddha's teaching: taking refuge in the Buddha, the Dharma, and the Sangha as a way to live in harmony with all things.

I continued to feel energized after completing the scrubbing, and the joy I experienced was based on not seeking approval from others but because I was coming from an inner natural state of joy. Scrubbing became an act of love and no longer doing a mundane task.

KEEP GOING
Roger Seiyo Cochran

The Dharma is the path that Gautauma Buddha explored almost 2500 years ago. He wasn't the first or the last to explore the path of seeing reality without judgment. The power of what he experienced was so great that its impact could be directly transmitted to those who studied under him without being written down, and Buddha's successors gave this direct teaching for 500 years before an "operator's manual" was written down.

I'm studying this operator's manual, the Theravada and Mahayana scriptures, and trying to sort out how to "use" it, as I read the various works in the Bright Dawn curriculum. And I'm also in another study group looking at how one of the heirs of Buddha, in Japan, Eihei Dogen, transmitted his understanding of how to operationalize Buddhism.

What I'm seeing is that the Dharma is not about a wishful projection of blissful life in a Tushita Heaven or some other pre-birth or post-death existence. Who can really know about those things? Rather, Buddhism, and the Buddhist Dharma, is about how to fully experience life right now in this life-time.

To me this is both liberating and terrifying -- liberating in that there is no vengeful deity to appease or any fear of an apocalyptic future to coerce my behavior right now, terrifying in that my chattering monkey-mind keeps me from the experience of life in this moment.

So my Dharma Glimpse is that this is like life itself. Life is to be navigated by myself in the midst of all other people who are making this same effort -- and in some way this is every person. Some are guided by fear of the past, some are guided by fear of the future. My own task is to recognize that the fears of others are not a sufficient reason for my own choices. But -- what "my own choice" is, is hard to distinguish since some of what I know is based upon the real world, and some of what I know is really based upon my understanding of the conditions and effects in which I was raised.

The only solution is one taught by Buddha, Dogen, and Rev. Kubose: keep exploring the self, continue being patient, see the deep problems that others face, and always Keep Going.

LIFES DUALITY IS ONE
Tamu Hoyo Ngina

Life is not always so easy
Life is not always so hard

May you see the rainbow
through every storm

May you see the love
through the harsh words

May each good thing that happens
serve as a lesson and as a blessing

May each not so good thing that happens
serve as a lesson and as a blessing

A LESSON IN MINDFULNESS
AND BEING IN THE PRESENT MOMENT
Linda Shoyo Wisniewski

About a month ago, I had a "costly" lesson in what happens when I am not mindful or in the present moment.

In *Living Buddha, Living Christ*, Thich Nhat Hanh writes: "Our true home is in the present moment. The miracle is not to walk on water. The miracle is to walk on the green earth in the present moment . . . . We only need to bring our body and mind into the present moment and we will touch what is refreshing, healing, and wondrous" (pp. 23&24). He also describes how the wonderful sound of the bell brings us back to our true home.

Well, it wasn't a bell that brought me back to the present moment but the sound of the sheriff's sirens and the lights that were the call to awaken and come back into the present. I really thought I had been more aware of being in the present moment -- except on this one morning. I facilitate a monthly book club, and I thought it started at 10:30 a.m. So, on that particular morning, I thought at 9:30 I still had plenty of time to take a leisurely shower and still get to the book club on time. Then I remembered that the book club started at 10:00 a.m., not 10:30.

Wow! I panicked! I was the one that had the questions for the book club, and in that moment I didn't even stop to think that I could call and tell a member that I would be late. No! I just became more and more mindless. I rushed getting dressed and started driving like I was really in an emergency. As I was going down the country highway I kept thinking, "Oh, I can get there if I just go a little faster." I thought, "Wow, I'm almost there!"

And then I heard the sirens and saw the flashing lights that seemed to come out of nowhere. And the man in blue came to the window and said, "I have to take your license. You were going 80 M.P.H. in a 55 M.P.H. zone, and that's the law." Well, the tears came because I knew I had to officiate at two weddings and I needed to be able to drive. Plus, living in the country, there is no way to get around without a car.

I guess the policeman had sympathy for me, because he knocked the mileage down to 78 M.P.H. so I wouldn't have to lose my license. He also gave me a $265 fine -- money I was going to use to spend time with my daughters in Chicago. And I was given six points. Twelve points in Wisconsin and you lose your license.

I also had the option to go to court and fight it. But I chose not to. Because, hearing the sheriff's siren was like a bell that quickly brought me back to the present moment; it was an expensive wake-up call for which I was in tremendous gratitude.

The present moment is where I find the peace and joy. It is truly, as Thich Nhat Hanh said, refreshing, healing and wondrous. He then went on to say, on p.24: to touch this peace, ". . . is not a matter of faith, it is a matter of practice . . . we need only to bring our body and mind into the present moment."

Since this incident, I really practice being in the present moment when I am in the car and just notice the beauty around me. I also observe my thoughts and how much, still, the thoughts are either focused on the past or future, and then I bring them back. It is a wonderful practice, and as long as I am in the present moment and mindful, I trust I won't lose my license or be stopped by those noisy sirens. The sound of a bell is so much more pleasing, and so is just being present.

LOOKING FOR THE DHARMA:
A GLIMPSE OF SOMETHING
Roger Seiyo Cochran

In my early 30's I had an experience that still seems transcendent to me. I was riding alone on a motorcycle through a rainforest where the local people were burning underbrush in preparation for planting crops. The smoke was dense and I could barely see the road under my feet and only vaguely saw the forest. It was as if I was traveling in a time and place not seen before. There was a sense of wonder, awe and majesty

But this experience has only rarely happened in the years since. I came to think of enlightenment as a rare experience.

But Bright Dawn has encouraged me to see enlightenment as daily life and to rethink my relationship to daily life, enlightenment and Buddhism. All of this has begun to make sense for me in the past two months when I've begun to see how being more compassionate in my daily life might actually be a gate to nirvana in daily life. So my Dharma Glimpse is pretty mundane, it is here today, in this act of typing up a Dharma Glimpse, because I'm paying serious attention in this moment. I'm attempting to let go of my attachment to how things ought to be and see things just as they are at this moment.

NON-ATTACHMENT
David Kakuyo Wisniewski

Lazy days of summer. Not! Hectic days of life are what it is for me. I do not like being on edge, waiting for another problem to force its way into my attention. Those that I can control some influence over mixed with actions beyond my control. A seeming whirl of doing and nothing gets done.

These are the thoughts that surfaced in my mind over the past weeks. I did not seem to be able to let them rise and then let them go. The idea that I had "been there, done that and got the "t-shirt to prove it" came to me in the morning. A peace came over me and things got a little clear. Life has no control, it just is.

I had been feeling like a pea in a draining sink going round and round toward the vortex leading into a dark pipe. It came to me that I did not know the difference between non-attachment and non-feeling and the underlying guilt I was carrying. I have really only within the past year been able to feel, to recognize things like hunger, joy, being at peace within. I had only known conflict or being alone. When this mind-picture popped into my head I realized that my old ways were automatically taking control. It is very easy to slip back when I take life as a thing to be controlled and not to be lived.

So what did I learn -- compassion does not mean taking on the other's problem, non-attachment is not being without feeling the pain of others, non-attachment is still loving my family and supporting their actions. Non-attachment is helping myself to really see the world around me and to see the wonder.

DANA
Dorothy Shinyo Merrick

Birthday Celebrations can bring out the best in people. I am a true receiver of this and my Dharma Glimpse today explains why.

Judy is one of my Condo neighbors. She is a few years older than I am and has two homes, one here in Florida and the other in Philadelphia. We have become good friends within the last year, when she's in town, and enjoy each other's company.

A few months ago, she told me she was doing something special for my upcoming birthday and because she likes to cook, I thought it maybe a cake or dinner or another culinary delight!

To my surprise, she presented me with a huge box. Inside this keepsake box was an afghan she knitted for me. The threads were soft and black (a color she thought would go with my decor.) The shell design was her favorite pattern. It was absolutely beautiful! Her card attached said that she made this afghan as if she was making it for herself, so attention to detail was a priority. She loved it, so she knew I would too!

She was correct. The time, energy, and love it took to hand-make a small blanket was overwhelming to me. How thoughtful. How meaningful. I was very moved with emotion.

By her generous actions, Judy became my teacher of a Dharma Glimpse. To give of oneself is the most precious gift one can give and I was a grateful receiver. This gesture is one that I can pass on also.

The next day, Pat (who goes to exercise class with me), had complained about a lingering cold. I decided to take out my crock pot and recipe for homemade chicken noodle soup, and by the end of the day, I delivered a container to her with a note, "While I'm no chef, this soup was made with ingredients that always make you feel better! Don't forget to salt and pepper to taste! - Dorothy"

She called me that evening to say "thank you and what a kind thing to do." She also enjoyed not cooking and ate it for dinner! Of course, this made me feel good, but most of all, thankful to a friend who helped me be mindful of giving. Thoughtfulness means so much more than words can ever say.

A VIEW FROM MY WINDOW
Linda Shoyo Wisniewski

Nugget: "Wisdom is to never stop taking a wide view of things."…."Our vision could widen to include the whole world."

I spend much time looking out the windows of our dome home. Over the 10 years of looking, it has been teaching me to take a wider view of life than what I could see out of only one window.

When I look out the large slanted window in the loft; I see only the sky and some passing clouds during the day; at night, the stars shine in and the moon when it's out shines through and seems to be circling around the dome. If I just spent my time looking out of this one window; in "my" narrow egocentric view, I would insist that the world just consisted of the sky, clouds, sun and stars.

But, on the main floor of the dome; we have 2 narrow rectangular windows that are close to the floor. Looking out of these windows gives me a view of fields of prairie grasses. From this view, I could say, these grasses mixed in with a few wild flowers made up the world.

PBS TV has a motto; Watching PBS is like having a window onto the world. i.e., their shows can give one a wider view of the world. But as demonstrated above, it can also narrow one's view and make me believe that what I see out of one window, is a true picture of reality.

Stepping outside I can see how all these separate views are all connected; It's teaching me to come from a wider view in the mind. I am learning that taking a wider view is really to cultivate a "beginner's mind." It also demonstrates that I really don't know on the surface what anything means; and if I think I do I am coming from ignorance. Truth reveals itself when we take a wider view than just seeing out of one window.

CAUSE AND REFLECTION
Mark Kaiyo Fives

One day this week, while I was outside at work reflecting on what I was going to use as my Dharma Glimpse, taking in the nature that was around me, I began thinking of interdependency, how many people, causes and effects went into creating what I was seeing: from the sun, wind and the rain sustaining all the trees, flowers and greenery, to the people who grew the flowers and planted them, the people who maintained them; the list goes on and on.

Then my thoughts shifted slightly to all the actions and reactions that have led to this very moment. The moment of me looking at nature, while at work, while thinking about my Dharma Glimpse, made me realize how special this very moment, and every moment, is. Everything we have thought and everything we have done, has led us to this very moment right here, right now. How can we not appreciate it?

ETERNAL NOW
Linda Shoyo Wisniewski

Ten years ago in September 2001, David and I moved from the big city of Chicago to the country. The nearest town is 6 miles away and we drive beautiful winding roads to get to it.

One week after we moved, the country went into a state of shock. fear and grief over the events of 9/11. Soon after we were involved in two wars which continue today.

I, myself, felt disoriented and couldn't reach anyone in Chicago or N.Y.C. where family was, and, I didn't know anyone here. I felt alone and fearful.

So, I decided to take a walk along the windy roads and stopped to watch the cows grazing in the fields. These cows, I observed were totally unaware of the events of 9/11 and what followed. I observed them being in the eternal now; no thoughts of the past, or future; eating when they were hungry; sleeping when they were tired; joining the herd when wanting to join; moving away when they wanted solitude; relieving themselves when they felt the urge; drinking water when thirsty; moving to the shade when it felt too hot and back into the sun after cooling down. Even on a rainy day, they grazed. The cow doesn't fear for his safety and life.

So this is what the eternal Now, Nirvana looks like, I thought. So this is what effortless effort, purposeless purpose might mean as I think about it now.

In the middle of chaos, watching the cows graze in the field reminds me that we are all in the eternal now; we are all in Nirvana. Life comes in the present moment, wonderful moment; I smile and am in gratitude. I feel so alive.

BAD COLD
David Kakuyo Wisniewski

A bad cold has been making the rounds where I work and, after all the care I had taken to protect myself, I have it. I am taking all the moves to lessen the effects but it will have to work its way through.

This is my Glimpse. I have a lot to do and I have no energy. Am I beating myself up because I cannot work, or because of the pain, or the dripping nose, or the low-grade headache, or because of the many other things that a bad cold brings? This surprises me, as I am not. I seem to have peace and acceptance.

It seems that what I have learned in the last months has changed my view or rather deepened my insight. This world can hold wonderful things as well as dreadful challenges. They are all part of life; each has only the importance I place on it. This will not end my life and if I worry and fret all I will gather is suffering. I have to live through the suffering and come out the other side as I really am. In time the cold will be taken care of and I can do the things I need to do. I find that I am not riding myself, telling myself I am a failure because I am not working at full strength. This time not even small echoes of fault are ringing in my mind.

I find a deep sense that my "self" is not made true by what I experience, but by how I see and feel that experience. I do not like nor do I hate this cold. It just is.

BEGINNERS MIND AT ANY AGE
Dorothy Shinyo Merrick

It was almost 2 years ago when my son and his wife had their first baby and my first grandchild. I remember thinking, "Grandma D (my new name) makes me feel old!" Yet, my son was 29 years old and I just turned 59 years young! I understand, this is the circle of life—children grow up, marry, have children and we grow old. So, what's wrong with being a Grandma? Is this my ego not wanting to let go of any feeling of youth or what?

While Age is still defined in years, I relate age with appearance, level of energy and an open mind to be flexible and adaptable to change. I am lucky to be of good health and have an active disposition by nature. The decision to remove the grey in my dark brown hair was easy. The abundance of catalogs I receive in the mail, keep me posted on the current styles; some appropriate for me and others not. Attention to living a healthy lifestyle has always been important because my husband and I believe a strong body promotes longevity of life, so then why is my mind rebelling?

Last weekend I had the opportunity to spend a few days with my granddaughter (Elle) while her parents went out of town to a wedding. She has language and comprehension skills now that amaze me for such a little toddler. She lives in the present. When she's hungry, she tells me. When she does not want to come inside from playing outdoors, she sits down in the grass and refuses to move. When she places the kitchen colander on her head and starts singing "Happy Birthday", it makes me laugh out loud!

All of this reminded me that **Children have beginners mind.** It is that wonderful attitude of openness, enthusiasm and lack of preconceptions when studying a subject and thus ordinary things shine. Beginners mind is precious. It can transform the way I experience life. My granddaughter demonstrated how it makes life exciting and fresh. By practicing the Beginners mind I can stay young and eager to learn. As I grow older, I can continue this while utilizing my wisdom acquired with age and experience.

Parenting or Grandparenting is a labor of love. It demands patience, understanding and tremendous sacrifice. Whether 2 years old or 61 years young, practicing the Beginners Mind will allow me to experience the moment fully. I am grateful for this time with her and look forward to the next.

WHO AM I: WHO IS THE SELF?
Linda Shoyo Wisniewski

Last week we worked on Koan's addressing non-attachment. The quote I used was "the strongest attachment of all is the attachment to one's self".

In meditation, the following came up addressing this. Initially I called it "Ode to broken Bones" but it really addresses the question "Who is the Self".

Aug 1st 2013, I awoke and looked into a mirror and freaked out. Who is that woman staring back at me? It's not Linda, Linda who prides herself on youth. Who's that woman whose neck is filled with wrinkles, whose back is stiff, whose wrist and fingers are swollen and in pain? Happy Birthday, you have now reached your 70th year and crossed the bridge from middle to "old age".

> *NO! NO! NO! Cried the 20 year old who could stay up all night and drink the boys under the table.*

> *NO! NO! NO! Cried the 35 year old, who as a single mother cradled two beautiful children, marched on picket lines and worked to put food on her babies' table,*

> *NO! NO! NO! Cried the 40 year old, who skied down mountains and camped outside under the moon and stars.*

> *NO! NO! NO! Cried the 52 year old, who just celebrated her 10th wedding anniversary with her second husband and body surfed the in the oceans of Mexico.*

> *NO! NO! NO! Cried the 65 year old, who still was working, plopping on the ground playing with 3 year old's and sharing information on growth and development with her parents?*

Who then was this wrinkled woman with creaky bones? Whose kitchen, all of a sudden, was filled with powders and pills to silence the achy bones and bunions?

Who is that woman whose children still go skiing and snorkeling? Who tells her children she can't because of her achy bones.

Who is that woman? Who am I?

> Am I my bag of bones or am I the song in my heart that can still sing at the top of her lungs in the shower. Am I the canvas which is painted with wrinkles and crinkles or am I the smile behind the wrinkle that lights up a darkened room.

Am I the achy old bones or am I the bubbly and cuddly woman who can still reach out and embrace you in a warm hug. Who can, with a loving word, dry all your tears?

Who am I?

I am the light, the moon, the stars, the good, the bad, and the ugly; the beauty and the beast; the bag of bones and the barrel of laughs.

I am all those things and none of those things. I am and that is enough.

On page 150 From "Zen Koans" by Rev Gyomay Kubose, he states, " growing old and aging are the realities of life and one must face them, regardless …Acceptance is Transcendence."

IN THE MOMENT
David Kakuyo Wisniewski

We have talked about being in the present moment at all times and I have tried many times. But when I do, the past and future come into my mind, the present goes away and worry, fear and past re-actions take over. It sometimes takes a decision to put all those thoughts away and take the plunge. This past weekend, I did just that.

We were with our grandchildren who were dancing to a dance video. When I was asked to join in, my first reaction was to say "NO" (but only to myself). Instead, I got up and started to dance to the song and moves on the screen. BIG surprise! I had fun and I liked laughing with the kids. At that time and place I was "in the moment" and the fear of making a fool of myself, of making the wrong moves and of showing the "inner child" was just gone. In its place was joy. This joy had no real place and no real time, it just was. Afterward, I got to thinking, "was this joy always with me and I never saw it or felt it before"?

WHY?

I always knew that I had two voices inside me and at times in my life I listened to one or the other. Was the "observer" silent, unknown and unrecognized by me finally coming to the fore? Is this feeling of joy a foretaste of what my life can become? I hope so.

So what did I learn? It is a choice that I make that colors the Now. I only have to let the present moment play out and let it be. Is this possible? If it is, what is it going to do to me? You see, the ego paints with fear and worry. Even now after this gift, fear comes to the front. Isn't life a wonder? I think I will "take the plunge" again and again and feel the joy. And fear WILL be left behind. I think the journey will be life-long.

RIGHT ACTION
Tamu Hoyo Ngina

Right action. Each and every day we are challenged in large and small ways to take the right action.

What exactly *is* the "Right Action"? This is the question that comes to my mind each and every time I think of the phrase.

Right action, for me, is the course I take when I choose, each day and even in crisis moments, to heed that still small voice within.

GATEWAY: First, harm none - Including yourself. And especially, other sentient beings.

Allow yourself to be fearless and to first trust yourself. Allow the answer that comes from within, the answer that is born from stillness in silence. That is the right answer.

No matter how life squeezes me all that will come out is peace.

CHALLENGING THE IDEA OF PERFECTION
Linda Shoyo Wisniewski

In our last session, Rev. Koyo stated we have to challenge the idea of perfection in our minds. This is something I have been thinking about, especially in the last few weeks when the pain in my neck has been getting worse and the swelling in my right hand intensifying. Since July, my fingers in my hand started to swell. Because I believed it could be healed solely through mind healing practices, I refused to go to a doctor until now, and I can't use or lift my right hand. This situation became a challenge when David informed me that the report I painfully typed out for last week not only didn't get sent along with his, but also couldn't be retrieved. I initially reacted with panic and rage--I can't type it over. It's just too painful. I might as well quit if I can't get my report in. I'm so exhausted trying to be the perfect student, the perfect spiritual person, the perfect minister, the perfect teacher, and the perfect healer. I noticed as I was in this rage the pain in the right hand was throbbing. I threw up what I was eating. When I'm in extreme stress, my esophagus shuts down and food gets stuck.

David gently reminded me: "it's not an emergency, it was an accident."

I noticed that I was in a state of panic based on fear from the past. In the present moment nothing was happening. Had I not been lost in the past it could all have been handled pragmatically with a simple phone call or email explaining what happened and no big deal.

Simply, to return to the present moment: I'm innocent; David, you are innocent. All is well. It is what it is. Now laugh and move onto the next moment.

So when I quieted down, I thought, why had I reacted with panic and fear and a belief that if I didn't do it perfectly, something terrible would happen? Where did the thought, "I've got to do it right – I've got to be perfect, come from?"

How does a mistake become a sin, i.e., a call for punishment? Why am I so hard on others and myself?

I know from my Jewish religious upbringing, there were these messages of we have to get it right in this lifetime. We only have this life to prove ourselves and leave a good name by the deeds we perform. Oh! I have to really question this concept. My father and brother were and are perfectionists and very driven. There was no room for errors or accidents. I was trained to live for the future. To judge all the actions I did on whether I would leave a good name upon my death. This is a hard way of living.

Now I've learned I have a choice.

Do I want to be right, or do I want to be happy?

Hell or heaven is not a place, but a state of mind.

I might not be able to control the world but I can control my reactions in every moment. It's my decision. It's really freeing to know I have very little or any control about how life unfolds except for how I respond in each moment. I remember the title of a book I once read: *Don't Sweat the Small Stuff and It's All Small Stuff.* It only took me less than an hour to return to sanity. But I hope the lesson I learned will last a lifetime. Perfection is not about past achievements or future hopes. Perfection is not about "efforting." Perfection comes in each moment.

I am being born anew in every moment.

It is so freeing to live this way.

POSTERS
David Kakuyo Wisniewski

About two weeks ago I came across a web blog site that posts many types of posters. I liked the motivational ones, and decided that I would copy some and post them where I work. My reason was I liked seeing them and reading them. They give me a lift, and at times I need a lift of spirit at work. Well in the past few days some of the servers started to read them (I leave posters up for a couple of days) and four of them made it a point to tell me how much they enjoyed them. Thursday, a girl I work with and thought I had no connection to, came in the bake room and gave me a calendar of motivational pictures and titles said, " I think you will like this and could you put it up."

I was floored, I had no idea that others would read them and that it would impact them. That the laughs and the "what is it trying to say" moment would reach them.

Since that time I came to realize that most or even all of the people I work with had made it a habit to come into the bake room to view and read the letter sized posters. What started out as a personal thing had grown into a work-place wide event. I had no plan that it would. The series of interactions and words between us has also grown into topics ranging from the simple into deep and meaningful exchanges.

This is another example of how I am interconnected with others, how my actions have touched others. The feelings of being happy and amazed and humbled that the world is connected and what I do affects all around me.

A side effect has been that this small experience has started me thinking, I can be an example for others and a very big example for myself.

A DAILY LESSON ON IMPERMANENCE
Linda Shoyo Wisniewski

Rev. Koyo gave me the idea for this Dharma Glimpse when every week he greets me with, how is the weather in Wisconsin? In one of his teachings he taught that uncertainty is a virtue. Well then, I guess Wisconsin and the entire Midwest is the perfect place to learn that lesson on a daily basis.

The capping phrase for living in Wisconsin or the Midwest is: You'll never know what the weather is -- it can change in the blink of an eye. The Code phrase would be: dress in layers.

Here is an example: It was March 2nd. This winter was really an amazing fluke; mild with only one major snow storm. We were all seduced into thinking it was a dream; we didn't know what to make of it. And, although we were joyful, there was a little bit of angst involved, wondering if we would get hit with winter in spring. Trying to enjoy the Now moments of unseasonably mild weather while not quite trusting what we were experiencing is a challenge. The egotistic mind doesn't feel comfortable with uncertainty.

So there it was on March 2nd; a clear bright 40 degree day. I was off to a day long retreat one hour from my home, driving my little Hyundai instead of the big 4 wheel Ford truck we use to navigate through the snow. All went well until 2:00 pm when out of the blue, giant snowflakes were falling fast and furious. Fear came up as I thought about having to drive home in my little Hyundai. But, I remembered the mantra, "present moment, only moment, smile". It was interesting also, that at the time I was walking the labyrinth, a meditative practice that is all about the present moment. So, by the time I got into the car, I was at peace in the present moment. And what a joyful ride it was. Even though the car nearly slipped over into a ditch, there was no fear. On all sides of me, a winter wonderland magically appeared. It was magnificent and awesome driving through the forests with the snow glistening off the pines. And, in a blink of an eye, it was over. The next day in 50 degree weather, the snow disappeared; an immediate lesson in impermanence.

Dressing in layers reminds me that as we remove one layer after another, we remove the artificial clothing that hides our natural state, our inner beauty, our true self.

That is what it is like living in the Midwest. Every moment there is a change in the weather. I could drive 20 miles and go from clear blue sky to a snow storm and from warm to cold. Yes, in the Midwest we live with continual uncertainty, but I am learning uncertainty is a virtue It teaches me that impermanence doesn't have to create anxiety; it can open us to the awe of just being alive in every moment, i.e. living fully in the Present Moment; living in truth.

LAY MINISTER CLASS #6

WHEREVER YOU ARE RIGHT NOW, STOP EVERYTHING
William Toyo Holland

(This is important)

Take just a moment and sit back in your seat.

Now, place your hands on your abdomen with your fingertips barely touching. On your next inhale separate your fingertips by breathing deeply and slowly into your belly, allowing your breath to push them apart.

Then exhale slowly so your fingertips come back together.

When you have finished, try it again.

There. That's it.

Namu Amita Butsu

To be continued………

TO BOLDLY GO
Douglas Sanyo Reagan, PhD

The Heart Sutra: To boldly go where you have never gone before...

The Heart Sutra is one of the prolific foundations of Buddhism, not only within the Mahayana tradition.

Shakyamuni Buddha espoused this teaching in the simplest form so that all of who heard it may clearly understand the richness of its meaning and comprehend its life lessons.

The Buddha taught the *prajna paramita* lessons for 21 years of his teachings.

It is seen as the 'heart' (essence) of the Buddhadharma.

Reflected in the Diamond Sutra, it is the most chanted sutra in Buddhist monasteries and temples in the world.

When I first read and chanted this sutra accurately, I felt as if I finally had a glimpse my true self.

Just as when I first saw a picture of the Earth from the Moon, I felt a connection to the vastness of the universe, and the pure awe of being a part of it.

When we landed on the moon, I was a child watching Star Trek. My admiration and fascination of Gene Roddenberry's vision didn't hinder this feeling, only inspiring me further.

Just as the Earth looks different from space, as it does when we are on the Earth; our sense and view of our own self is very different to what we perceive.

The Heart Sutra is the view of the enlightened mind and enlightened eyes, just as our enlightened view from space upon this planet.

Like the missions of Star Trek, we seek to explore an unknown universe within a realm of human actions, emotions, and frailties.

The word **sutra** in Sanskrit means 'thread'. Something that binds together. The root for the word *suture* comes from this.

The Heart Sutra binds the *prajna paramita*, the innate Buddha's sacred wisdom... the **truth** to all living things.

To force us to see with the enlightened eye, and to develop the enlightened mind and heart.

Just as a single candle cannot illuminate an entire building, the light of wisdom (*maha*) can, like the sun, illuminate the entire globe.

The *prajna paramita* is the supreme wisdom that enlightens us to the highest of goals, to cease samsara, and to awaken to the enlightened nature... the true nature. The wisdom of the Buddha.

Paramita is defined as 'crossing over'. Going to 'the other shore'. To go from suffering, to nirvana.

Maha Prajna Paramita – To go from suffering to enlightenment by our innate wisdom.

Nirvana therefore is not something that we must seek outside ourselves, but from within.

It is the meaning of the Greek word *Utopia*, which means a place of no suffering and no worries about being provided for. In reality, we are far from this in the world, and within ourselves.

Examine the beginning sentences of the Heart Sutra, "When the Bodhisattva of Great Compassion when practicing *prajna paramita*, realized that all five aggregates are empty, and became free from all suffering." When he realized the nature of the human condition... his true self -- then he was enlightened.

He explored a 'strange world', and he went to 'where no one had gone before' – and reached the complete truth... enlightenment... nirvana.

When we see our true self, which is very different from our conventional belief, then we can become free from our delusion,

> To be our true self,
>
> To awaken the Buddha nature within,
>
> To be a Buddha.

This is the essence of the Buddhadharma. To be truly free from our fears and dissatisfaction.

When we know our true self: this is Buddhism -- this is living the Dharma -- this is Nirvana.

We accomplish this from our study of the sutras and meditation. Through our living as awakened beings, by living the Dharma, and thus being an example of the *prajna paramita*.

To paraphrase, "My real self... the Final Frontier. This is the continuing mission of the Buddhadharma. To explore a strange new world. To seek out my life and the true essence of civilization. To boldly go, where I have never been before."

Namo Amida Butsu

©2013, Douglas H. Reagan, PhD

FIREFLIES
Michelle Jouyo Sullivan

Friday was the first day of Spring. Almost as if they knew this, the fireflies chose that day to make their first appearance at our local park. We've been watching for them for the past week, knowing that they usually show up this time of year, and the temperature has been perfect for them – humid and in the 80s and 90s pretty much every day.

There are about 2,000 different species of fireflies, and they all have a signature flash pattern. This flash acts as a mating signal, as a way to tell one species from another, as a way to tell males from females, and as an indication of which males are more desirable to mate with.

Their appearance to do their little mating dance on the first day of Spring was a fantastic metaphor for what Spring represents – renewal and rebirth. But these little beetles are also a perfect metaphor for the cycle of birth and death.

You see, fireflies have a very short lifespan. They live just long enough to mate and lay eggs. Some never even eat during their adult phase.

While our own lifespan is not as short as that of a firefly, it is still relatively short. I am coming up on the one year anniversary of my dad's death. He was only 67. The year before that, one of my uncles died at the age of 48. And right now, while I'm watching the fireflies dance their dance of life, my last uncle is in a hospital bed dying at the age of 60.

Death is an interesting thing. I think we all know that it is coming, but we have this abstract idea that it will come to us peacefully, in our sleep, when we are old. That may even happen for some of us, but it won't happen for all of us. We don't know *when* our time will come, but we have to remember that it eventually *will*.

We are just like fireflies, dancing and mating and producing offspring, blissfully ignorant to the fact that one day, we too must die. We're trapped in the same cycle of birth and death. The difference is that we know how to stop that cycle. By practicing the Dharma we can take refuge in the Deathless. The Buddha once said in a sutra that we should all practice as though our turbans were on fire. Perhaps we should use this Spring to practice as though we have the lifespan of a firefly.

YELLOW PAD MEDITATION AND THE PURSUIT OF HAPPINESS

William Toyo Holland

Writing is a form of meditation and a passion that brings happiness into my life. I have this love affair with yellow legal pads. I write all my letters, essays, quotes, Dharma Glimpses, poems, and yes even a haiku now and then on this wonderful tablet. Before I get into the root of my Dharma Glimpse, here's a short history of the yellow legal pad.

The legal pad got its start with Thomas Holly in 1888. The legal pad's margins, also called down lines, are drawn 1.25 inches from the left edge of the page. This is the only requirement for a pad to qualify as a legal pad, though the iconic version has yellow paper, blue lines and a red gummed top. There are a few competing hypotheses about how the pads came to be yellow. I will go with the one story that suggests that yellow was chosen because of the colors "stimulating effects" on the person's intellect and contrasted well against black ink without a glare, making text easier to read.

I keep each and every one of my pads, even though the words eventually end up on a hard drive and saved as a file of some type. Have you ever known people who sing in the shower, I seem to always form expressions and ideas about Buddhism while in the shower, hurrying still dripping from the shower to find the nearest yellow pad to record this flash of wisdom. This is why they are yellow so you can find them easily.

Over the years you can imagine or maybe not, the boxes and stacks of legal pads that have been accumulated. You will find them lying everywhere, I'm just the type of person who hates to throw anything away, clinging, attachment, who knows. Even in college I preferred the legal pad over a loose leaf binder. I find happiness in my yellow pads and writing gives me a sense of balance and awareness.

Happiness is a practice. It's on us to learn it. Benjamin Franklin said: "The constitution only guarantees the American people the right to pursue Happiness. You have to catch it yourself."

I find that writing in general is a challenge of the mind and the practical approach to the essential teaching of Buddhism. It is bringing ideals into our everyday lives and how to put these ideas into practice. Writing down all my thoughts and mindful experiences is very rewarding. My writing, I find, is essentially very effective in promoting a happy, peaceful life. Loving what I do each and every day is important. I always spend a few minutes thinking of all the bits of life that I am grateful for. The art of writing is the art of discovering what you believe.

By writing, it gives me a way to carve out a path to a bright future and to also share some key areas of the Buddhist way of life in clear, simple but thought-provoking language. This can also be an excellent introduction to often-over-complicated traditions.

I do not in any way consider myself someone of great wisdom, but I do have a great compassion and commitment to educating people to think and act in a spiritual way and hopefully passed on to others. All of this does not come automatically. It is not a gift that good fortune bestows upon us and a reversal of fortune, takes back. It depends on us alone, one does not become happy overnight but with patient labor, day after day Happiness is constructed, and that requires effort and time. And maybe a shower and some more yellow pads.

In order to become happy, we have to learn how to change ourselves. When we keep practicing, the changes you will see in your life will be mind-altering and will alter your life. For some happiness comes easy, no thought or routine required, for others, simple reminders and practices are all it takes.

Happiness is a choice, it always will be. Grab a yellow pad and find some happiness. This is my way as a Bright Dawn Lay Minister to create "Human Happiness."

I remember reading "To be truly happy is to finally end the search."

Breathe in the brilliance of this day and let all of its wild colors stun you!
And make sure to take time to see every little thing.

KANTI – WHEN SOMEONE SPIT INTO BUDDHA'S FACE
Roberto Keiyo Velez

I have been reading about the violence in Myanmar and it makes me sad that Buddhist monks should be committing acts of murder and arson. Truly, we are witnessing the decline of the Buddhist Dharma, and I hope that there will be peace there and that monks can somehow go back to the precepts. Please let's send metta to the golden land of Myanmar and for those Muslims who have died or who are in fear for their lives; may peace be with them all.

The Buddha was conversing with his monks when a man walked up to the Master and spit right into his face. The master gently cleaned his face with his robe, looked up at the man and asked "do you have anything else to say to me"? Ananda, his close attendant, jumped up and scolded the man. "Master," he said, "we cannot let this man do this; he must be punished or else others will come and disrespect you. We should make an example of him!"

The Tathagata said to Ananda, "This man has not offended me but you have offended me with your words." Ananda bowed to the Buddha and said, "Master I don't understand." The Master then faced all in attendance including the man, "This man is a stranger and others have said to him that Shakyamuni is an atheist, that he leads people away from religion, takes people and makes them follow him to beg, causes families to suffer when their children seek him out, and that he is an evil demon." When I asked him what else he had to say, it was because he spoke from his heart without words and this way of speaking is always powerful, it proceeds before thinking and is to the point; this form of communication is full of emotion and force. This man did not spit on me but rather he spit on a notion of who he thought I was and he spit on the mind's impression of what it thinks I am.

The man quickly turned and ran out of the place where the Buddha was sitting. When he got home he found he could not eat and when he tried to sleep he could not find peace as the words of the Master spun in his head. When the light of day peeked into his home he rushed out to find the Buddha, and upon getting to the grove where the Tathagata was sitting he ran up to him and throwing himself down he put his head on the Master's feet and cried out, "Forgive me lord, forgive me." The Buddha reached down and picked up the man and said, "Now, now there is nothing to forgive." "But yesterday I spit in your face, my lord!" said the man. The Buddha turned his lotus eyes to the man and said, "The man you spit on yesterday is no more. He is gone and the one who did the spitting is also gone. They no longer exist. Now why don't we sit and talk?" And they walked away and sat.

This is how the Buddha forgave and it has a lot to do with Kanti. Now when we read in the sutras about Kanti it is translated to mean Patience. This is just one of its meanings. The other is to let go of the desire for retaliation and revenge, which to me is the same as forgiveness.

If we look at many of the sutras, we very seldom read about forgiveness. But to me this is most central to living a Buddhist life. It is not easy to forgive. Many of us have learned from the theistic traditions how godly it is to forgive. The gospels and the whole of Christianity are based on this premise, "If God forgave us, then we should forgive others." Sometimes this is known as the Golden Rule.

The function of forgiveness in Buddhism has a different flavor in that having and cultivating the practice of Patience is a paramita or perfection. Now if someone harms us intentionally that's one thing, but it is even harder when someone unintentionally without their knowing it hurts us. You see, to forgive is to let go of hurt, to give up grudges. The extending of feelings of good will to those who offend us is forgiveness, to those who oppress us, to those who hate us, who regard us as enemies. Forgiveness is an act of self-transformation. When we forgive, we transform negative mental states into positive mental states, which is the heart of the Metta sutra. Now does that mean forgive and forget? Well, we really cannot forget the memory of the event. It stays in the mind to remind us not to succumb to people or events that can hurt us. But with that in mind, if it is safe to do so, then we should forgive.

Well, suppose you cannot forgive for other reasons that would put you in a vulnerable position. Try writing a letter never meant to be sent, in which you write out your forgiveness and then burn or destroy the letter. I cannot remember how many arguments my wife and I have had but we know enough to drop it and continue as before, knowing we will never agree with everything. Seeing eye-to-eye does not work all the time. Holding on to resentment, revenge, retaliation, and the I-hope-they-suffer-just-like-I did scenario is like planting weeds in your flower garden. The weeds will kill and choke the tender flower sprouts. Look at the world in the age of the terrorist where hate along religious lines has created so much pain, hurt and hate along racial lines and still rears its ugly head. The great Buddhist Saint Shantideva wrote "The mind can find no peace, nor can one find calm and delight, nor can one sleep well or feel safe while the knife of anger and hatred is stuck in our hearts. Those we honor in this world with honor and respect and even one's own family and best friends will stay away from us. The one who realizes that hatred is our enemy and strikes it down, will be happy in this world and in the next."

Forgiveness is a no-brainer, you know. To have a real enemy is rare. I mean think about it, a real enemy lives just to see us suffer and die. Only a real enemy has the time and resources to carry their hate out, once more Shantideva says "It is the best good fortune to have a real enemy because they provide us with an opportunity to practice real patience and forgiveness. No one ever prevents us from doing good and even if they do, it is still an occasion to practice Kanti, for Kanti is the greatest of virtues."

As for myself I hope that if I have hurt any creature through action, word or thought that they may find it in their hearts to forgive me for my ignorance and I, in turn, forgive those who cause me harm. Peace be upon you all. Let's practice Kanti and grow in the light of Amitabha.

HOW TO COLOR OUR DAY
William Toyo Holland

The other day the press was interviewing Lucy Li, the youngest qualifier in U. S. Women's Open history at the age of 11. She has been playing golf for half of her life. Heading into the tournament, Li said her only ambition was to "have fun and play the best I can."

She played well the first round but did not make the cut the second round of play. At the press conference she confirmed that she really wasn't concerned about the outcome at the end of the day, she just wanted to have fun, enjoy the game and live in the moment standing on a crate and eating an ice cream cone, strawberry I believe, my favorite. A reporter asked her what she was going to do to prepare for the next tournament. She replied, "eat more ice cream."

This is a great lesson. We often spend too much time worrying about what the results are going to be at the end of our day, about the future and the past and not what is happening here and now. Lucy Li, might have to work on her cravings but don't we all. I'll be right back. I'm going to the freezer now to see if there is any ice cream.

Not being in focus and in the present moment reminds me of a lesson I learned running the S.F. marathon many years ago. I was so concentrated on finishing in the top percentage, I was totally unaware of what was happening around me. I realized afterwards that it was not fun, I did not enjoy the race. Even though I ran my personal best! My Awareness and Mindfulness was absent, I was not living in the moment.

Mindfulness I believe is a kind of energy that helps us be aware of what is going on within us and around us or the practice of moment to moment observation of the present moment with a non-judgmental, non-discriminative mind. While the practice is simple and clear enough, there are numerous objects that we can observe and some difficulties may come up in the process of observation

I woke up that morning with invisible blinders on. I was not really aware of the runners next to me. My ears were muted, I wasn't listening to the sounds around me, I was totally focused on the finish line. I did not think about how grateful I was to everyone and everything that made it possible for me to be there in the first place. The list would be endless.

One important ritual we should add to our spiritual toolbox is to remember to remove these invisible blinders, once our feet hit the floor in the morning. By not doing this, we can often experience our day in black and white, in the absence of the wonderful color of awareness, mindfulness, compassion and loving kindness. Which is after all the cornerstone of Buddhist practice. I call this coloring the way we approach spiritual practice.

Most of us have rituals that help us start our day on the right path, and to keep us mindful throughout the day and to help us cope with all the demands. These rituals can help us learn the art and science of mindfulness practice and how to show compassion.

Compassion can be shown in many different ways. A very simple way to show our compassion is to leave the bathroom clean, so that the next person who comes finds a wonderful place. We don't leave a little note there saying, "I did this for you." It's just done, and there is that clean place.

I'll end by leaving you with a small tip! The next time you find yourself struggling or in trouble, just look up into the sky for a few minutes. You will feel a lot better when you return to earth.

I am very grateful to the Bright Dawn Sangha, for giving me this opportunity to share this Dharma Glimpse and again reach into my spiritual tool box and continue my journey.

HAPPINESS
Richard Doyo Hamling

And for everything else… there is Master Card, the story goes.

We often hear and see how others have designed our happiness. Why are we so easily duped?

There are nearly 17,000 book titles on happiness. I wonder if ever-lasting happiness can be found in a book. Why are there so many books on the subject? Happiness seems to be part of the struggle in being human. Some have come to think of happiness as a literal right, like a tangible object, something to grasp and hold, never to be lost.

My car is like a personal Zendo at times -- a place to be quiet with my thoughts and a place to stumble into new thoughts that may breathe life and meaning into new and old experiences. At times this is my Walden.

I travel to a psychiatric facility periodically for an administrative meeting. It can be a lengthy drive sometimes two hours for a meeting lasting only an hour. It is a valuable driving time, through the scenic Finger Lakes region of New York State, passing a glacier formed lake of nearly seven hundred feet deep and well known for quick storms and the loss of lake visitors, often going unfound due to its structure and frigid waters. On this day a man in a small boat was fishing. What courage he must have to take such opportunity. I don't think I could do it, I thought. Everything has something to teach us when we have the courage to notice. There is a price, however, of risks and rewards.

As I drove, I thought about the many opportunities we have day to day, moment to moment, to have spaciousness of mind, an opportunity for reflection, to notice whatever we have is contained within the moment. This happiness or sadness is fleeting. If we try to hold it too tightly, we cannot fully experience it. If we fail to notice, we fail to give rise to an opportunity of growth or richness in our existence. Is this what is meant by being fully human or alive?

Soygal Rinpoche, within this context, tells of how to contain a herd of cows is by giving them a very large pasture. The Dharma gives us the pause in dualistic thinking to have a pasture as well. The Dharma provides the break from dualistic conditioning to create a pasture, a speciousness of mind that opens and offers possibilities different from our standard way of being in the world. It requires us to let go and be open to what is, to formulate concepts more spaciously, not rigidly bound. Sensei Kubose speaks of, "letting our hearts and minds become as vast as the sky." Further, Sensei states, "this goes beyond an intellectual perspective" or getting out of our heads. Existential psychoanalyst Rollo May and psychologist Abraham Maslow describe this as an awe or peak experience. There are risks and rewards in personal and spiritual growth.

There is, indeed, much more to life than happiness and despair. We sell ourselves short by only wanting one or being rid of the other. How happy can we be when we confine our thoughts and beliefs?

Happiness arrives when we come to accept its nature of fleeting or impermanence. Same for despair, it is temporary, despair will come and go.

There is life. Our task may be to find contentment in this most basic truth. Our constant striving to be happy actually is counter-productive. It is a sure way to be miserable. If the goal is all that matters, we are grossly and continuously disappointed, only wanting more that is endlessly not enough. Happiness is, after all, an inside job; otherwise, we live to achieve one goal after another, never fulfilled and living ill at ease.

In our goal directed society, this is a hard point to live and teach.

I had a student many years ago in an introductory counseling course who was very unhappy with her B-grade for an essay assignment. She was adamant that an A was necessary because she "only gets A's. She could not be satisfied with anything less than an A. I suggested she do the assignment over. A week later she returned. Still, the assignment did not meet an A standard. She was so unhappy and increasingly angry with me. I gave in and gave her a B+. This did not satisfy her need. I asked her to do the assignment over. Angrily and reluctantly she agreed. A week later after class, somewhat confidently she presented the paper. It was better, but... I shook my head. She started to cry, yelling, "What do you want. I'm an A student, what do you want?" She was an A student everywhere, but with me. She went on ranting then said, "f** you Dr. Hamling. I know what I know!" She calmed down. "Let's start over," I said. "What did you learn from the assignment," I asked. She said she learned "how falsely we judge others and... ourselves, in doing so she was unhappy and miserable, not being able to enjoy what life had to offer." At that point I said, "<u>Now</u>, you have an A!"

A life of acceptance, seeing deeply into things as they are, not artificially, we open up all to all of our experiences and capacities for happiness, sadness, contentment; this is easier said than done, but what are we without this?

PET RELATIONS AND OUR BUDDHA NATURE
William Toyo Holland

It's not very hard for me to relate to animals, as my father was a wildlife biologist and growing up my home was inhabited at times with quite a variety of animals.

To name a few, a small man-made pond was home to a pair of otters and a beaver that ate the leg off my mother's kitchen table. Others included a squirrel monkey, a raccoon, a skunk, turtles and lots of snakes and even an orphaned bear cub for a short time. And of course, birds and dogs.

I was given my first dog on the day I was born and I have always had one or more by my side almost all of my life -- a wonderful dose of happiness each day.

I would often find myself in hot water in grade school by having a critter of some kind in the comfort of my pocket or hidden in my back pack. I also was the originator of live designer ware, with a pet lizard tethered to my shirt collar, and my teachers were always wise when I would wear my shirt tail out. Yes, I was the kid that put the toad frog in the teacher's desk drawer.

Pet relationships are an important part of our lives. Our relationships with our furry friends have great influence upon our wellbeing and happiness.

A dog is a pack animal. Social by nature, it needs to be involved with its human family members or its canine friends. It needs to feel a part of the family. It wants and needs relationships. To deny a dog its emotional needs or treat it like an object, devoid of emotion, is to emotionally abuse the animal.

We can also apply this lesson to our personal relationships. We must always be aware of our partner's needs.

Life lessons do not always come the easy way but if there is one place you can find them, it's through your pets. Our pets teach us to live simply, love generously, care deeply and speak kindly. The Buddhist way, is it not? Embracing the idea of living like your pets can open up your world, help you savor every moment, and enjoy every day.

This all brought into view what I thought were the three most important lessons learned from my canine friends; Forgiveness, Compassion and Awareness. We all should pay a lot more attention to our animals and learn Compassion, Awareness and Forgiveness from their well-being.

We all know the infamous and most debated Koan, "Does a dog have Buddha-nature or not?" The answer being "Mu" literally meaning that dogs do not have Buddha nature, and has been interpreted to mean that such categorical thinking is delusion and that 'yes' and 'no' are both right and wrong.

Well, let me be the first to confirm, without a doubt that dogs, along with every other living creature, have Buddha nature. Part of the Buddha's enlightenment is said to be his realization that all beings have Buddha-nature.

And this is why I say this!

Dogs are the most advanced beings on the planet. They are fully self-realized. They possess unconditional love. They forgive instantly. They are empathetic and sympathetic. They are incapable of guile or dishonesty. They're always in the moment, not carrying the past or fretting about the future.

Everything's always new and wonderful. Every place is always the best place to be. If you think about qualities you'd like to possess, the ideal qualities - unconditional love, loyalty, devotion, unwavering friendship, forgiveness, selflessness, sincerity, being fully present in the moment - qualities we uphold as the loftiest ideals to which we might seek, they look very much like, you know, a good dog: dog consciousness.

By those same ideal standards, humans are far and away the least evolved beings on the planet.

Do dogs have a Buddha nature?

Dogs are Buddha nature. We don't need books and teachers and philosophies.

If you want to learn from a great spiritual master, get a dog, they're the real Zen Masters.

So, are you looking for a little 'Zen' in your life? Get a dog! or two!

Bijoux and Dante send their blessing.

Namu Amita Butsu

A TREK IN THE PRESENT MOMENT
Douglas Sanyo Reagan, Ph.D.

"Resting near a small waterfall, Picard and Anij sit on rocks, the captain staring through binoculars at their destination: caves set into distant mountains. Just ahead, the babbling of the waterfall silences as the water becomes a fine mist, flowing more like sand than water. Picard wonders how Anij is able to do this, but she has no answer for him. They sit in silence and enjoy a 'perfect moment' in which time slows and they are together."

In this poignant scene from *Star Trek: Insurrection*, we are witness to a wonderful example of the Buddha's teaching: the miracle and beauty of the present moment -- the moment of wonder, of sublime clarity, and our fullest sense of oneness of ourselves within the universe -- when all is still, calm, and in virtuous harmony with all things. The Dharma teaches us that this awareness is an achievement of enlightened beings -- the moments when all things become clear.

Picard gazes awestruck at the hummingbird stilled in flight; they sit in silence, absorbed in reflection of the sublime beauty and clarity of their surroundings. Picture yourself in that location, in that situation, the stresses of life removed and the unification of one's self with all that is. This example of stillness -- of our minds, our hearts, and the fact that we may see the core of our existence -- is reflected in Anij and Jean-Luc's tranquility and peace.

Examples such as these should remind us to always live and be in these precious-yet-fleeting moments. Happy and joyful, we are able to visualize ourselves free from the ties of samsara. When we still our minds, we are calm, at peace, and centered within the universe...as it really is. We remind ourselves of the true purpose of this life: to be free of the continuation of our suffering.

The perfect moment, the present moment, is all that really is. The past has come and the future yet undetermined. May we all become awake to the present moment, to live in harmony with all beings and to treasure the many moments we have in life. Regardless of what those moments contain, let us remember to often be still and observe the pure beauty that surrounds us all -- once a day and every day.

Namo Amida Butsu

MUSTERBATION
William Seiyo Shehan

How many times a day do you Musterbate? Does Musterbation control your religious practice?

First let's define "Musterbation." It is a term coined by Dr. Albert Ellis, who is considered the father of Rational Emotive Behavior Therapy. The term refers to demands that result in self-defeating behavior such as, "I must, we must, she must…"

While Dr. Ellis talks about it, in dealing with society's problems and even health issues, I want to talk about how I see it applying to Buddhism.

If you tell a friend that you are a Buddhist, as you have a shot of whiskey, or take a bite of a nice steak, they will most likely start asking you "How can you…." This is Musterbation. The assumption that if one is Buddhist, they MUST be calm, be a vegetarian, have some Eastern heritage, be a hippy, and the list goes on.

Now take a moment and think about what you think a Buddhist must be. Now take a moment and let that go and just be what you are, not what you think you MUST be.

TURNING POINT
Roberto Keiyo Velez

Since I first began my journey on this path I have had the time to think back on what I believe was the turning point in this brief life. That is what I would like to speak on today.

What was that point? It was my repentance for all the stupid and hurtful things I did in my past and the ones I will likely commit in the coming years. We talk a lot about the Dharma and we look at different aspects of the Teaching, but so far I have not heard about repentance except in the section we did on Naikan. It is one of the most important aspects, if not the threshold to the practice.

In all of the world's great religions repentance is the cornerstone of living a true change of life -- the practice of self-examination in which we can see where we have not lived up to our true potential. In the taking of one's moral inventory we see the lack (what we have done and what we have failed to do is one of the prayers in the Catholic Mass) of compassion and loving-kindness. The guilt and shame spurs us to reexamine our lives and move forward in the right direction. At the same time, this guilt and shame is the cause for much of our mental defilements and mental illness when it becomes a stumbling block towards living a fully integrated life.

Now Gautama Shakyamuni was born into the warrior class and so he had a moral code that was instilled in him that if he did harm and acted in a way not consistent with that code, it would bring shame to his clan and that was unthinkable. So we can assume he would never even think of doing something un-warrior like. So his moral compass was set to live in accord within the caste he was born into. Like young Gautama, the act of living to a higher calling has brought us here today.

There are many ways for one to show how sorry one is for the slips one has made in this life. In Buddhism, there are rituals which allow us to unburden these mental chains so that we might put them behind us and allow us to keep going. In this society there is a dislike for that term REPENTANCE. Why should we be sorry for what we have done? I always hear the saying, "to err is human," and I'm only human after all. In the last book we read together on the practice of Naikan, repentance is seen as a practice we should indulge in frequently as we look deeply inside and see where we are heading. In the Theravada tradition the monks, at least once a month, publicly repeat whatever faults they have committed against the Vinaya (the code of ethics in the sangha), and it is the job of the Abbott to give counsel. There is no absolution in this tradition. Who can change the karmic actions once committed! The Sangha is asked to send Metta (loving-kindness) to that person (and to you, my brothers and sisters, to pray for me to the Lord our God, would be the equivalent in the Catholic Church).

The other wheel of the repentance cart is forgiveness, where we not only seek reconciliation with those we have hurt but also with ourselves, for the cart which the two wheels uphold is our self-image which can take a long time to heal. Personally, I have undergone therapy for many years to learn to accept myself as I am, just as I am. The health system in these United States has a long way to go when it comes to mental health; there should be an amendment that we should all have the right to free mental health counseling regardless of socio-economic background. Until this happens, I think we need to reflect on the two wheels of this human vehicle, repentance and forgiveness, if we are going to have a stable and enlightened country.

THE ETERNAL BUDDHA'S DESIRE
Douglas Sanyo Reagan, PhD

I was recently asked "what is the desire of the Buddha for me"? I explained the aim of Buddha's desire for all living beings is for all of us to end our delusions, to obtain enlightenment, and to become a Buddha ourselves. This is common to all schools of Buddhism.

Our life of delusion is due to our selfish desires and not living in accord by what is true and real. We are constantly repeating our faults and by doing things our own way, we cause ourselves and others to suffer. This always results in more problems, or can compound other difficulties. However, there is a way out of this cycle of delusion.

The Buddhadharma aims to correcting our selfish nature and offers all living beings the path to enlightenment. When we acquire true wisdom and compassion we are able to see everything in its true nature and perspective. This is connecting to the "Buddha nature" that resides within all living beings. This allows us to treat all things with equanimity, with a compassionate and true mind.

All the Buddhas transmit the true mind with compassion. The Buddha's desire is found in the Dharma which allows us to be free of the fetters of our own delusions, increase our compassion, and fully live with wisdom in unison with the changing nature of the universe itself. This is the totality of our life by practicing the Dharma. By doing so, we help not only ourselves but all others.

When the Buddha's desire manifests, we receive it within the Nembutsu, like that of a warm and gentle heart. Just as the name of someone dear to us, so too is the name of Amida Buddha just as dear. Bringing the special feeling that we share with those special people in our lives, we achieve the same feeling by reciting the Nembutsu and thinking of Amida Buddha. This is different than simply saying any other name because of our cares, problems, and difficulties. Because we feel and connect to the Buddha nature within ourselves, our hearts are connected with the eternal Buddha. This is how I feel about the Buddha's desire for all, in Oneness.

Namo Amida Butsu

A BRIDGE TO ONENESS
William Toyo Holland

For the last year and a half I have been watching a bridge being built near my complex. It was completed this past month. It is a short bridge about the length of a football field. The construction of this bridge drew my attention to what bridges bring to us and their connection to Buddhism. After all, Buddhism has a lot of bridges if you think about it. Also, in Rev. Koyo's book *Bright Dawn* he expresses that on our spiritual journey, a bridge helps us travel from the shore of ignorance to the shore of wisdom. A bridge is a concrete way to express the movement of crossing over, and any significant experience can function as a bridge whereby one can "cross over," becoming a different person and living a new life.

Bridges can be an exclamation point on our spirituality. They also may be transformational as a way to break through mental blocks that we sometimes face. Bridges can completely change your frame of mind. They might bring in visions and personality in ways that you might not otherwise experience.

Meditation is a bridge we cross that allows us to travel within ourselves to find the truth. We can also use chanting as a bridge to help us cross over to the other shore. A bridge is a structure allowing persons or vehicles to proceed over obstacles like rivers, valleys or gorges. A spiritual bridge will let us proceed over obstacles that are in our spiritual path. The Buddha mentioned building bridges for the public good as an example of a meritorious deed.

Crossing a river is frequently used as a metaphor for the spiritual endeavor in the Tipitaka. In Buddha's time it was known that people and horses vied to board small boats that then capsized, drowning their passengers. We have learned from Buddhist teachings that bridges were constructed to prevent the suffering, harm and even death of travelers.

The Buddhist enthusiasm for building roads and bridges had a significant role in developing trade, communication, the spread of Buddhism and lessening of the hardships of life. Records show that building bridges as a religious practice became very popular in China and Japan. The Japanese monk Dosho was famous as a road, dam and bridge engineer.

One of Japan's most famous pre-modern bridges, the elegant Spectacle Bridge in Nagasaki, was designed and built by the monk Moku Sun You Jo in 1634. This structure was the first stone-arched bridge in Japan and is still in use today. It was given its name because when its two arches are reflected in the water it looks like a pair of spectacles. Coming back to the present, I've been known to get carried away with historical text.

I do know that that my encounter with two different bridges in the past not only started me on my spiritual path but had quite an effect on my life and compassion for others, and started me on my journey with Buddha (Buddhism A Way of Life). The first was in 1965, when I marched across the Edmund Pettis Bridge in Selma, AL with Martin Luther King Jr. and thousands of other non-violent protesters. This was when the Buddhist term Dukkha arose within me. Not being a Buddhist lay person at that time, I was still very much aware of the suffering, hatred and pain and even death that was so prevalent at that time of civil unrest in the South. I knew in my heart that I needed to be a part of this movement and draw attention to the suffering and pain of a race that was being discriminated against. I am sure that the Amida Buddha crossed that bridge with all of us that day. Today this would be called a bridge to Engaged Buddhism, which is a growing and important part of Western and American Buddhism.

The second bridge brings me even closer in contact with Buddhism; this was the Golden Gate Bridge. The Golden Gate Bridge became what I like to think of as my path or bridge to Buddhism. I began my journey and Zen training in San Francisco when I journeyed across the Golden Gate (even the name seems to have a spiritual reference to it). I was on my way to join my fellow Buddhists at Green Gulch Farm and Zen Center located near Muir Beach. This is where I met Shunryu Suzuki, Allen Watts, and Zentatsu Richard Baker and many others that influenced my Buddhist path. Living in the city I also jogged across this bridge each morning and often times looked down to see thousands of small white caps dancing on the water below, and I let my imagination see thousands of little Buddha's giving me safe passage to the other side.

In life we often find ourselves crossing bridges, rather than being mental or physical, and we can add them to our spiritual toolbox. This is all part of a ritual practice that we can develop. Instead of just crossing the bridge to get to the other side, we must always be aware of each moment and be grateful for the bridges that we choose to cross and allow us to get to the other shore.

The Rev. Gyomay Kubose used his spiritual bridge in transmitting the essence of Buddhist thought, as Rev. Koyo continues to do the same today with the Bright Dawn Center of Oneness Buddhism. Bright Dawn is now another bridge I can add to my travels and spiritual journey.

A quote from Thich Nhat Hanh: "Breath is the bridge which connects life to consciousness, which unites your body to your thoughts. Whenever your mind becomes scattered, use your breath as the means to take hold of your mind again."

I will leave you with a Haiku or maybe even use it as koan:

Although there is a bridge,
My horse goes through the water.

May it be so !!!! Namu Amida Butsu

STUFF
Michelle Jouyo Sullivan

George Carlin had an entire stand-up routine built around "stuff." He said that your house is basically just a place to keep your stuff.

Well, my husband and I decided recently that we'd accumulated entirely too much stuff over the years and really needed to get rid of a lot of it. We thought we might as well try to have a yard sale to see if we could get a little money out of getting rid of things, and anything not sold at the end of the day would go to the Habitat for Humanity thrift shop.

We spent a Saturday sitting in our driveway surrounded by enough stuff to fill a large U-Haul, wondering how on earth it had all fit into our house to begin with. Not that many people even stopped, and the ones who did mostly just looked around and then left. We sold very little, so when we decided to just pack it up and call it a day, we contacted the Habitat store to come pick up the rest while we brought the books to donate to the library. When we got back the Habitat store had been there, and had actually left some stuff behind.

We couldn't even GIVE away our stuff. So why had *we* been holding on to it?

How often do we find ourselves holding on to the "stuff" that clutters our minds? When we hold onto things like ego or anger, clinging, restlessness, doubt, or boredom we are cluttering our minds the same way our stuff clutters our house. We aren't leaving room to cultivate mindfulness. We are holding on to things that we don't need and that others don't want. If we could just step back and say, "I need to empty this space," we are taking the first step in clearing ourselves of the clutter that prevents us from developing skillfulness.

Think about it – if your room is cluttered, you can't really see what you have in the room. Maybe you are looking for something, but it is behind a pile of books or it is stuffed in a junk drawer. So if your mind is cluttered, how clearly can you see it? If you can't see past the stuff to what's going on in your own mind, how can you cultivate wisdom, or happiness?

The Buddha said, "Monks, one who has not fully known and fully understood aversion... delusion... anger... contempt, who has not detached his mind from it and let go of it, is incapable of putting an end to stress. But one who has fully known and fully understood aversion... delusion... anger... contempt, who has detached his mind from it and let go of it, is capable of putting an end to stress." (*Itivuttaka: The Group of Ones* § 10-13. {Iti 1.10; Iti 5})

Part of the path to the cessation of suffering is to rid our minds of these mental processes that we cling to and carry with us. We managed to clear out some stuff from our house. I like to think I also learned a lesson in clearing some stuff from my mind.

KOANS, DREAMS and WHAT REALLY HAPPENED TO THE CAT
William Toyo Holland

"Your Vision will become clear only when you can Look into your own heart. Who looks outside, dreams; Who looks inside, awakes."

Carl Jung

During the week, I try to get my mind set and focused on how I want to approach my writing and practice and it works most of the time. I also like to listen to music when writing, today I choose Sawyer Fredericks, winner of The Voice.

The other day at work, I was moving some paper drink cups and underneath a paper placemat I found that someone had written in ink, "Do horses get songs stuck in their heads." Well it got stuck in my head and I could not imagine who would have written it, or even where it originated from. I went to bed that night with it still stuck in my mind. In the middle of the night I woke up from a dream; Gene Autry was riding his horse Champion across the prairie, singing Tumbling Tumbleweeds, which happens to be one of my favorite cowboy songs and may be a Dharma message or two.

> *See them tumbling down*
> *Pledging their love to the ground*
> *Lonely but free I'll be found*
> *Drifting along with the tumbling tumbleweeds*

Well do horses get songs stuck in their heads? I said "MU" and went back to sleep.

One more thing that I do each week is to pick a koan or a haiku to ponder. This week I choose Nansen Cuts the Cat in Two. Reverend Gyomay M. Kubose says; "Unless life is understood, this koan never will be."

We really don't know if this is even an accurate account of what really happened or if Nansen really cut the cat in half. And why were the monks arguing over the cat, maybe since the cat demanded a lot of attention and during zazen it would curl up on their laps which broke their concentration, like my dogs at times. Or maybe they were just arguing about whether the cat had Buddha nature or not, or debating what is a cat anyway.

This story is just like the more shocking biblical version: A tale of a human baby threatened with being cut in two to settle an ownership dispute. Surely the real mother will cry out that the imposter mother should take her child rather than see her child come to any harm. The imposter, not possessing that affinity and nurturing impulse, reveals herself. The child is then given to the real mother who cared enough to relinquish her attachment to it.

Maybe, just maybe, no cat was actually harmed in the making of this Koan.

Also this could be all about Joshu and a pair of sandals. In fact I am thinking of the next time Marsha and I have a misunderstanding or argument, I'm going to take off my shoes and put them on top of my head and walk out of the room! As with Marsha's reaction, I think that after watching Joshu walk away with his sandals atop his head, Nansen may have thought something along the lines of 'That is the most ridiculous thing I have seen all day!'

There are a lot of ways to interpret this and all koans. I do find it myself, to be a good mind exercise. As we know, koans are meant to assist in shocking the mind into awareness or enlightenment.

Do you remember this passage:

> *"To study the way is to study the self. To study the self is to forget the self. To forget the self is to be enlightened by all things."*
>
> Dogen Zenji

SCRUFFY
Michelle Jouyo Sullivan

We had a visitor to our house a few weeks ago. Our visitor came to us in the form of a stray dog that my husband picked up at the park. She was apparently old, very scruffy, and badly in need of a bath...or ten.

She smelled like she might have rolled around in trash, eaten it, vomited it back up, and rolled in it again. We bathed her, and it took three shampoos before the layers of dirt coming off her were no longer the consistency of mud. And she STILL smelled bad. She was missing teeth, had infections in both eyes, and was badly infested with fleas.

But she was also incredibly sweet and really wanted affection. Whenever we came near her, she'd jump up to greet us. I loved this dog after only having her with us for less than a day. We knew we wouldn't really be able to keep her, because she really deserved a home where she could get lots of attention. We have two very high-maintenance dogs already who act like attention seeking missiles. So, we took a photo of her and posted it to Facebook, seeking either the owner or a good foster home. We got many inquiries, but after learning that she would be a "project dog" – a dog badly in need of some serious vet care and potentially carrying unknown illnesses – most people just backed out or stopped returning our calls. They were really looking for a cute little dog, and it wasn't obvious from the photo that she might be old or sick.

Many times, without realizing it, people treat each other the way they treated this dog.

We go through our lives sometimes not realizing the impact that we have on others. We tend to gravitate toward vibrant, lively people who look and seem healthy and attractive. We often turn our backs on the scruffy people of the world – the homeless, the poor, the old, or the sick.

In fact, we like to lock many of these people away where we don't have to look at them, as though hiding them somehow makes the fact of them go away.

When you spend any amount of time cultivating the Brahma-Viharas – loving-kindness (metta), compassion (karuna), empathetic joy (mudita), and equanimity (upekkha) – you learn that you can no more turn your back on the "scruffy" people of the world any more than you can turn your back on your own suffering. We start to recognize the true meaning of Oneness.

What gives us hope is that there are people in the world who spend their lives tirelessly working to help those who can't help themselves...those people society has chosen to forget.

Just as these people exist, so did someone who actually wanted to take on Scruffy. She went to a good home, and the couple who took her had already made arrangements for care with their vet. We were able to let her go knowing we'd left her in good hands. She had a happy ending – it turns out she wasn't very old at all; in fact, she was a purebred dog who was microchipped, but the chip was never activated. She didn't even have any major health problems, either – just the eye infections and the fleas. It turned out she just needed a little TLC and she's now thriving under the care of her new family (they don't call her Scruffy, by the way – they've named her Punkin).

LESS IS MORE
William Toyo Holland

Lunar eclipse
Moon missing
Venus looking on.

Himalayan wine
Darjeeling tea
Empty cup.

Walking with Thay
Forgot to breathe
Mindfulness retreat.

Fog in mind
Keep going,
It's just the weather.

"I am"
Oh, I'm thinking
Narrow mind
Empty space.

Kathmandu trembling
Stupa in ruins
Buddha still standing.

Mosquito at my ear—
Does it think
I'm deaf

Ocean calm and set
View of sunset
Gray pelicans soar

Bright rays of sunshine
Shimmer on the ponds surface
A turtle finds warmth

Spring pond deep and wide
I listen to cicadas in the willow
The lotus is sleeping

Sweet corn, dressed in silk
Strawberries on the way
Soliloquy

LAY MINISTER CLASS
#7

THE TRUE MEANING OF ALOHA
Marge Shakayo Elwell

Moving to Hawaii was an enriching experience. My home on the mainland was always on the California coast (in my adult life). I lived a full and active lifestyle. I had a research lab in Malibu and a home in San Clemente. There were 180 stop lights between labs (a nightmare). When the time came to retire I brought up the requirement that wherever I lived there would be NO stop lights. O.K. My husband Dennis found this quite beautiful place called Ka`u (a.k.a South Point) on the Big Island of Hawaii. The landscape was a green forested area on the slopes of Mauna Loa. The culture was multi-faceted due to the different customs of the labor force brought in for the sugar plantations.

My first encounter of the word ALOHA came from my real estate agent. Being of an enquiring mind I started to research the meaning. Todays Glimpse will cover a very broad meaning. The breakdown goes something like this:

> A = AO
> L = LOKAHI
> O = OIA`I`O
> H = HA`A HA`A
> A = ALOHA

A = AO

Light. We must remember that our behavior must always look in the direction of light. We should always lead ourselves, as well as others, in the direction of enlightenment, and with watchful alertness.

To look. HO`O AO means: to look for the appropriate time and place, to be mindful of what is around you, inside as well as outside of yourself. If we are talking, that means we are not listening. There are some people who like to hear themselves talk and talk and talk and to overwhelm us. You should look around to see if it is the right time to speak out loud or not. Interesting people have a lot to say, but is the audience ready for what you have to say?

L = LOKAHI

All is one: Oneness. We need to support the people that are with us on the Path. Anything less than 100% support is sabotage. Oneness requires being **PONO** and **ONE** with everybody. PONO means proper balance; if you have some issue with me, come and tell me. The process can be done inside oneself and outside in person. Get together, and talk it out (KUKA KUKA). If you are "inside" then you can't look at the other person to see if you're PONO. This is why it is very important to know how to LISTEN and look across rather than talk and look inside. It is one step closer to Oneness. My parents were Roman Catholics but they taught their children the most important part of marriage and friendship was not to part as enemies or with anger but with understanding and light.

O = OIA`I'O

I'O = truth. Tell the truth. This is not easy. Most of us want to tell the other person what we want them to hear. If we don't tell them the truth we are defeating the purpose of PONO. We are not participating in the whole process nor constructing a solid foundation for Oneness to develop. When we are holding things back we are not allowing complete participation in the process of Aloha.

H = HA`AHA`A

It means to be humble. Ha`a ha`a is being aware. **EGO** IS A VERY BIG TRAP. The minute you think you know something, you may be ruined in spiritual manners. The only reason you are not telling the truth is because of ego. If you continue being a "know it all" or playing the game of "showing off" then you'll always have to know more than others. What a waste of time and human compassion. YUK! On the other hand, the more you are putting out there, the more you are sharing. So timing, place and knowing your audience are very important. Whatever you do you must remember to be **HUMBLE**. If you come across as being a KNOW IT ALL, you will be spending a lot of energy proving yourself, and perhaps losing the best part of Aloha, the "A".

A = ALOHA

Absolute, true love. As soon as we think to start judging people it starts a wedge separating us from true love, the spark of true divine essence, compassion, the true spirit, the essence of true sharing in the universe.

The Spirit of Aloha was an important lesson taught to the children of the past because it was about the world of which they were a part. One early teaching goes something like this:

Aloha is being a part of all (Oneness), and all being a part of me. When there is pain, it is my pain. When there is joy, it is also mine. I respect all that is a part of the Universe and part of me. I will not willfully harm anyone or anything. When food is needed I will take only what is needed and explain why it is being taken. The earth, the sky, and the sea are mine to care for, to cherish and protect. This is Aloha!

Remember when you say "Aloha" it means "Hello" and Goodbye", and most all of "Love".

Namu Amida Butsu

PERFECTION
Kyle Kaiyo Williamson

This last weekend I was babysitting my nephews, and we decided to work on an art project. The older one wanted a gloved hand like his favorite super hero, Iron Man; the younger one just wanted to be a part of the fun. So I traced the older one's hand and began cutting out the tracing. I then handed the cut out over to him, and he colored it in red and gold crayon.

When we tried tapping the cut-outs around his hand, we found they did not fit exactly. He became distraught. Unfortunately, he threw a tantrum and was sent to time-out. When I checked in with him to see why he was so upset, he stated that the hand was not perfect.

I tried to explain to him that it doesn't have to be perfect to be fun, because our imagination is what makes it fun.

His comment made me think about the disappointment I feel when things aren't 'perfect'. Be it a meal that turns out sub-par or a dinner party running late, I am easily discouraged when things don't turn out perfect—that is, the way I want them to be.

I find it amazing that as early as 5 years old we find ourselves frustrated with a lack of perfection. Buddhism believes that the source of this frustration stems from our assumptions and attachments. If we think something should be a certain way, there is no room for flexibility when the reality does not meet our mental assumptions.

Perfection is an idea in my mind; it is not reality. I need to reflect on this idea and try to free myself from my assumptions about how things are and my attachments to how things should be. The frustration and disappointment that I experience are all self-imposed. This suffering is avoidable if I follow the Four Noble truths.

In _Ocean:An Introduction to Jodo-Shinshu Buddhism in America_, Kenneth K. Tanaka says, "People who expect life to be 1) smooth, 2) 'mine' 3) always the same, and 4) lousy, have unwholesome views. They are going against the Four Marks of Existence. To help us remember this, I say 'Think BIIG!' but 'Don't Think SMAL!' (smooth, mine, always and lousy)" (Tanaka).

I'd gotta keep going and 'Think BIIG" not "SMAL"!

BUDDHA'S FLUTE
Ajita Choyo

Thus have I heard: The Great Sound of Right Enlightenment vibrates and flows throughout the Cosmos. The flute is an ancient symbol for this Great Sound, aka Omkara or Pranava. I would like to look at the flute symbol within Buddhist iconography in this Dharma Glimpse.

The flute is the oldest instrument discovered by archeologists, and the most ancient flute found thus far is dated as being between 43,000 and 45,000 years old. The flute appears cross culturally as a spiritually charged symbol linked to the ever creative, transcendent yet immanent, Universal Spirit/Breath of Life. Here is some Buddhist iconography in which the flute appears.

A = "Depiction of Krishna playing flute in the temple constructed in AD 752 on the order of Emperor Shomu; Todai-ji Temple, Great Buddha Hall in Nara, Japan". "Krishna appears as the 'Dhammasenapati' or 'Chief General of the Dharma' and is usually shown being Buddha's 'right hand man' in Buddhist art and iconography." "The 'divine boy' Krishna as an embodiment of wisdom and endearing prankster forms a part of the pantheon of gods in Japanese Buddhism." http://en.m.wikipedia.org/wiki/Krishna#Buddhism

B = Bodhisattva on a cloud playing a Flute. A Celestial Musician, called 音声菩薩

"Bosatsu of Sound" おんじょうぼさつ. 1053 AD carved wood. The Byodo-in Temple, Japan.

C = One of the 28 statues who are the Guardians of the Buddha at Sanjusangendo temple in Kyoto and obviously a Japanese flute playing form of Garuda.

D = Benzaiten, the Japanese Buddhist form of Saraswati, playing the flute (although this form is less prevalent than those where she is playing the Biwa).

E = A Chinese bronze statue of Kwan Yin (aka Kannon, aka Avalokiteshvara) playing the flute.

While it is possible to think of the flute in the hands of a deity as a symbol of that deity's creative power, it is also possible to think of the flute as one's personal heart being held by Deity, a heart in which the Transcendent Soundless Sound resonates. But only a heart which is first made empty is suitable for divine music-making. Becoming empty one can thus become filled with the fullness of the melodious Song of Infinite Life. The Sufi tradition teaches that the pains and sorrows which the heart experiences through life are like holes made in a reed flute which then allow the Divine Song to be produced within one's heart. To put this in Buddhist language, deep insight into life's sufferings makes the heart like unto a flute, which when open to the Reality of Emptiness, can then be used as the Buddha's instrument, for the transformative music that He ever wishes to create. No earthly instrument can produce the music which the self-emptying heart experiences. When I enter into meditative absorption I hear a high pitched ringing sound like that of a flute. There is deep peace and reassurance in this inner sound current which carries me aloft and keeps me going.

I would like to share a Vaishnava tale about Krishna and Radha (the Supreme God and Goddess), and about Krishna's flute being the great spiritual teacher:

Radha asked Krishna: "O my dear! Why do you love the flute more than me? What virtuous actions has it done so that it can remain in close contact with your lips? Kindly explain to me, my Lord, the secret of this. I am eager to hear". Sri Krishna said: "This flute is very dear to me. It has got some wonderful virtue. It has emptied off its egoism before I began to play. It has made its inner hollow quite void and I can bring out any kind of tune, Raga or Ragini, to My pleasure and sweet will. If you also behave towards me in exactly the same manner as this flute, if you remove your egoism completely and make perfect self-surrender, then I shall also love you in the same manner as I love this flute". https://answers.yahoo.com/question/index?qid=20110206084925AAgya1d

May all beings gain deep insight into life's distress and, perceiving Emptiness, transform sufferings into openings for the Great Sound of Right Enlightenment to vibrate and flow in all directions.

HRIH AUMTAT SAT

ASK THE RIGHT QUESTION
Ken Kenyo Haile

... when you ask the right question you get the right answer ...

In a Jim Henson movie, the creator of the Muppets, titled Labyrinth, a girl named Sara is trying to rescue her baby brother (earlier she wished that he would vanish—see how our wishes come back to haunt us?) She must traverse a labyrinth to get to the castle to reclaim her lost brother. On her way, she meets a gnome-like character named Hoggle. Here is their conversation:

> [15:08 minutes into the movie]
> **Sara:** Excuse me but I have to get through this labyrinth ... can you help me?
> **Hoggle:** (Ignores her.)
> **Sara:** Do you know where the door to the labyrinth is?
> **Hoggle:** Oh Maybe ...
> **Sara:** Well where is it? ...
> **Hoggle:** Where is what?
> **Sara:** The door!
> **Hoggle:** What door?
> **Sara:** It's hopeless asking you anything!
> **Hoggle:** Not if you ask the right questions.
> **Sara:** (pauses ... gives some thought ...) How do I get into the labyrinth?
> **Hoggle:** Ah, now that's more like it. You gets (not a typo) in there. (He points to the door and the door opens.)

Sara did not know how to enter the labyrinth. She asked Hoggle a question that she thought would give her the answer. But, it did not work. First, she had to learn HOW to get the information she wanted. In this short scene, when Sara asked the right question she got the information she needed.

One of the most difficult challenges I've met is learning something completely new to me. I do not even know how to begin to ask questions to get the information I need. I have to keep guessing and rephrasing my questions until, like a key, I finally manage to unlock the door to the knowledge I seek. Once the door is open, I can progress, step by step, building a structure of understanding. This process eventually takes me to the knowledge I seek.

I believe that my Buddhist journey has been like Sara's. In many cases I've not known HOW to ask the right questions. I've only been guided by a desire and "hints" along the way. Like Sara, some might say, "Why keep this a secret, just give me the information!" However, I have discovered that much can be learned from the process of creating the question. In some cases, the answer is revealed as I work to phrase the question. The process of forming the question prepares one to UNDERSTAND the answer when it is given. Without this preparatory work, one may never recognize the answer that comes later.

A great movie plot that I have enjoyed is the existence of a "wise person" who is not recognized as such. The answer to the question is eagerly sought by the actors, while overlooking the solution which lies right in front of them in the form of a wise person. Finally, after many trials and failures, the wisdom of the unrecognized sage begins to unfold. When they finally ask him/her/it, the riddle is solved.

In my intellectual pursuits, I am sometimes frustrated by not knowing. I feel like I am not progressing. This feeling shows a lack of understanding of the value of the process of forming the question. Forming the question is what prepares me to recognize the answer. Then, like the movie demonstrated, the right question will finally reveal the answer.

OPENING THE NINE BUDDHA QUALITIES
Ajita Choyo

The nine qualities of the Buddha are commonly chanted in the Theravada Buddhist tradition.

1. **Araham:** The Accomplished One

2. **Samma sambuddho:** The Perfectly Self-Enlightened One

3. **Vijja-Carana Sampanno:** The One Endowed with Knowledge and Virtue

4. **Sugato:** The Well-Spoken One

5. **Lokavidu:** The Knower of the Worlds

6. **Anuttaro Purisadammasarathi:** The Supreme trainer of persons to be tamed

7. **Sattha devamanussanam:** The Teacher of Celestial and Human Beings

8. **Buddho:** The Enlightened One

9. **Bhagava:** The Blessed One

Because I have a special affection for the power of sacred words, I wished to find a way to incorporate these nine names of the Buddha into a personal ritual. The first thing that came to my mind was the way in which Vaishnavas mark their bodies with tilak while chanting various deity names. (http://www.harekrishnatemple.com/chapter6.html). I also thought of a quote by St. Paul in Ephesians 6:10-18.

"Finally, be strong in the Lord and in the strength of his power. Put on the whole armor of God, so that you may be able to stand against the wiles of the devil. For our struggle is not against enemies of blood and flesh, but against the rulers, against the authorities, against the cosmic powers of this present darkness, against the spiritual forces of evil in the heavenly places. Therefore take up the whole armor of God, so that you may be able to withstand on that evil day, and having done everything, to stand firm. Stand therefore, and fasten the belt of truth around your waist, and put on the breastplate of righteousness. As shoes for your feet put on whatever will make you ready to proclaim the gospel of peace. With all of these, take the shield of faith, with which you will be able to quench all the flaming arrows of the evil one. Take the helmet of salvation, and the sword of the Spirit, which is the word of God. Pray in the Spirit at all times in every

prayer and supplication. To that end keep alert and always persevere in supplication for all the saints."

I was led to briefly explore various cross cultural purification rituals. *(http://en.wikipedia.org/wiki/Ritual_purification)* I found it interesting that in Japan there are ritual basins for purification, before entering a Buddhist temple, which often have a spiritual poem inscribed on them. The poem inscribed on the tsukubai at the Ryoan-ji temple reads "ware tada taru (wo) shiru", which translates as "I only know plenty," meant to convey the meaning that "what one has is all one needs."

(http://en.wikipedia.org/wiki/Tsukubai
http://www.japanesegardening.org/reference/tsukubai.html)

And so the idea came to me to create a Buddhist ritual of marking the body at various points, with perhaps sandalwood oil and in a circular Enso pattern, while intoning the nine qualities of the Buddha. According to Wikipedia, "Sandalwood is considered to be of the padma (lotus) group and attributed to Amitabha Buddha.

Sandalwood scent is believed to transform one's desires and maintain a person's alertness while in meditation. It is also one of the more popular scents used when offering incense to oneself."

(http://en.wikipedia.org/wiki/Sandalwood#Buddhism)
[For more information on the nine qualities of the Buddha see http://www.tbsa.org/articles/BuddhaQualities.html or http://www.usamyanmar.net/Buddha/Article/The%20Nine%20Qualities%20of% 20Buddha.pdf. And for information on the chakras, see http://en.wikipedia.org/wiki/Chakra, or just use Google to pull up many other sites.]
Here is the ritual I created: (for personal chanting purposes I slightly altered the ending forms of a few of the traditional Pali words.) I would begin with however one takes the Triple Refuge and then proceed with this rite.

A RITUAL FOR AWAKENING THE NINE BUDDHA QUALITIES

WITHIN:

Anoint at the first chakra while intoning "Buddho"
Anoint the second chakra while intoning " Bhagavan"
Anoint the third chakra while intoning "Anutarro Purisadammasarathi"

Anoint the fourth chakra while intoning "Araham"
Anoint the fifth chakra while intoning "Sugato"
Anoint the sixth chakra while intoning "Lokavidu"
Anoint the seventh chakra while intoning "Sammasambuddhaya"
Anoint the sole of the left foot while intoning "Sattha deva-"
Anoint the palm of the left hand while intoning "manussanam"
Anoint the sole of the right foot while intoning "Vijja-carana-"
Anoint the palm of the left hand while intoning "sampannong"

I'M NOT FROM MISSOURI ... BUT ...
Ken Kenyo Haile

I like to look at license plates from different states. Due to the small size of the plate and the requirement that its numbers be large, each state has a limited opportunity to boast of their advantages and, sometimes, attempt to convince you to visit and spend your vacation money with them. Some states recognize this and do a great job with an attractive plate and a slogan that encourages you to do a little more research to discover its meaning. Others do an impressive job of missing this opportunity.

The state of Missouri has the slogan "show me state." You'll find that there are a number of interpretations of this slogan. I had learned that this meant that it is important to see the evidence of a claim or to "Show Me" the proof before you accept the claim. The story goes that a Missouri Congressman, Willard Duncan Vandiver, followed a speaker whose claims he doubted. He said "I come from a state that raises corn and cotton and cockleburs and Democrats, and frothy eloquence neither convinces nor satisfies me. I am from Missouri. You have got to show me.[1]"

It has been my life's lesson that, no matter how experienced or educated one may be, they can make mistakes. Human fallibility is a trait we all share. As the saying goes "To err is human ...[2]" What is risky is to believe that one, by special egoic dispensation, has been spared this trait of humanity fallibility. Just because some "authority" said it does not mean that it is true.

One morning I was asked to repair a problem with a computer. Without having investigated the situation, an "expert" informed me of the cause. Though I took his recommendation into consideration I first tested his claims. I found them to be false. My preliminary investigation yielded a solution in about 5 minutes as opposed to the "expert's" proposal – saving me about 25 minutes of unnecessary activity. Mid-way through my repair he again passed by and mentioned that another part of the computer was not functioning. With the same flippant air he proposed the "obvious" solution.

Once again, I tested his assumptions and found them to be incorrect. Once again, I had solved the problem in about 5 minutes instead of wasting another 25 minutes doing something unnecessary.

I return to my original thought of "show me." "Experts" and their egos fight forcefully to prove their own infallibility. Generally, they are not comfortable living on the fringes of "not-knowing." This may be perceived as weakness.

Making mistakes is not necessarily bad – it is a part of our humanity. However, we must guard against influences of the ego to think that we are infallible. Humility, sensitivity, and awareness to this tendency may save us lost time and energy pursuing goals or ambitions that will not be fruitful. When we are so obsessed with "knowing" that we will pretend we know, we deny ourselves the opportunity of seeing "what is." We must continually prove to ourselves and others what we think we know. We must also cautiously prove the truth of what others propose to us.

Many and varied are the practices of the path of Dharma. I believe that we have a personal responsibility to question the practices and beliefs of these "experts" to insure that their counsel and authority do indeed result in the benefits claimed.

1 http://www.netstate.com/states/intro/mo_intro.htm

2 http://www.phrases.org.uk/meanings/to-err-is-human.html

RUNNING WITH THE MIND
Kyle Kaiyo Williamson

I have recently learned a valuable lesson about my mind and the need to run with it.

I was carrying my partner's phone as he had left it in the bathroom, when the text alert went off. I was curious and my partner and I allow each other to read through each other's phones allowing for complete disclosure. (Some people may find this odd or an invasion of privacy but for us this just works.) The text was confirming that he was leaving work early to take a friend to their tattoo appointment.

I knew nothing about this and my mind went into hyper speculation drive. Is my partner getting a tattoo with this other person? Is there something going on here? Why didn't he tell me about this? He doesn't have to tell me everything but we usually share anyway. What is he hiding, more importantly why is he hiding?

From a little information I speculated a variety of possibilities ignoring the most likely possibility; my partner didn't think this event was that important. Since I can't be a victim in this scenario, nor can I be a hero, my ego immediately dismissed this possibility.

With my emotions running high and my victim-hood established in my mind, I confronted my partner. "Why did you hide this tattoo excursion from me? I would never hide my plans from you." He of course became defensive about my accusations and explained that it wasn't a big thing he was taking some PTO to take a close friend to get their tattoo, to show support. He had no intention of hiding it, he simply hadn't thought about bringing it up in conversation as the plans had just recently been cemented.

I was running behind my mind and following wherever it ventured. If I had taken a moment to think through my reactions, "Why is he hiding this"?, I probably could have realized that he really didn't think anything of it. More importantly I could have handled the situation better by simply asking him about it instead of accusing him with my question.

We have since resolved this issue but I am so embarrassed that I let my mind run away.

I am ashamed that I caused suffering for myself and my partner over a delusion, a mental fantasy. I had been running behind my mind when I need to, at the very least, run with my mind.

So what does running with mind entail? What does it look like?

For myself this requires taking those speculative reactionary thoughts and holding them against some logical test. Does this thought make me either a hero or a victim? If the answer is yes, this speculative thought is probably reactionary and I need to be very cautious of it.

Running with the mind also involves taking the time to focus on my SPOT (Special Place of Tranquility) - Thank you Koyo Sensei for this acronym! Sitting and deeply listening allows me to go from my mind's co-conspirator, to its observer. Observing the irrationality of my mind helps me to understand how important the hero and victim test is.

But to do any of this I have to MAKE THE TIME, I have to schedule this into my TO DO LIST.

Running to the grocery store or to the gym must be equal in importance to running with the mind.

The goal of running with the mind is to increase wisdom and compassion while decreasing suffering the result of which is more happiness. Remember:

HAPPINESS = (Reality) − (Expectations/Assumptions)

GO FOR BROKE
Ajita Choyo

"Go for broke" was the motto of the 442nd Infantry Regiment, a World War II Japanese-American military unit, and is a phrase from Hawaiian Pidgin meaning "to wager everything." I use it here as my Dharma Glimpse title both to convey the "keep going all out in spite of everything" philosophy of our Bright Dawn lineage as well as a personal reassurance that in our brokenness is found our wholeness, also part of the Pure Land teaching that endarkenment must come prior to enlightenment.

The personal context of my Dharma Glimpse this week is a recent romantic heart-break. Although I am middle-aged and have had a broken heart before, I have not experienced such depth of anguish in the past. This is most likely due to an expanded sensitivity to emotions which I have developed in mid-life, being largely stuck in my head for a large part of my early life. As I am training to become a Bright Dawn lay minister, and have studied and practiced spirituality for many years, I feel somewhat like a hypocrite because I am suffering so intensely from this emotional attachment and having a hard time adjusting to this life transition. But hopefully because of this experience I will be able, in time, to mature in my Dharma practice and be able to minister to others more effectively.

I do not feel the need to go into the specifics of the situation, as the experience of heart-ache is common to us all. Understandably I have been feeling a mix of emotions, including fear, anxiety, regret, depression, anger, et al. I feel off-balance and incapacitated by this turn of events. I am deeply disturbed and dumb-founded. Gassho! It is a synchronicity that this has occurred during our study of koans, because I sense the knotted tension in my core that has appeared is itself a koan to meditate upon. I suspect that when one takes a koan seriously, such a knot appears in one's hara. I can tell myself, "Acceptance is transcendence". I can ask myself "Where is your troubled mind?" I can urge myself to be grateful for what we did share in the past and can share in the future. I can know that others have gone through much worse tragedies and survived. I can watch the changes of sensation and perception in my mind stream. But none of these things ease my pain it seems. I figure since I have to do a Dharma Glimpse this week I may as well do it on what I am experiencing.

So I am making use of this experience to reflect upon the Dharma. I try to picture this knot in my stomach as the Endless Knot, one of the eight auspicious symbols of Tibetan Buddhism, connecting and leading me to Truth.

I hope to uphold the honor of our lineage by overcoming my own mind-made obstacles to happiness. I aspire to abide in the Brahma Viharas. Yet the road to each vihara is blocked by my own clinging mind. My situation is not one in which there is a clean break, no black and white, but one of living changing color tones in which certainty does not exist. Of course it did not exist in the past either. I only assumed it did and this ignorance was pleasant feeling. Without an easy exit out of the relationship altogether, transitioning to a different and uncomfortable relationship form appears to me a super-human task right now. But becoming a Buddha is a super-human aspiration and what I signed on for. Just writing this essay, embarrassing as it is, is therapeutic. When I hear my critical internal dialogue, such as "I will never love or trust again", I must remember the limitless of Amitabha and that we manifest what we think. I have to laugh at myself for thinking my happiness is only in and through the power of another person, rather than happiness being my natural state. Many aspects of my relationship with her are now changed but one cannot know how any relationship will change in time.

So what is the wisdom I can gain and share from this unwanted koan whack? I am not sure, but I am being challenged to deepen my commitment to attaining and abiding in the Brahma Viharas. I trust that I will be able to minister to the broken hearted on a deeper level now that I have personally felt this depth of heart-ache. I am not going to deepen my despair by indulging in sex and drugs and other forms escapism, which I know would make me feel more isolated and alienated. But I can appreciate why people may try such avenues of escape.

I guess my Dharma Glimpse message is that the only way out is through and that there is no need for my feelings to be other than what they are. My composure and patience are being tested and hopefully purified and magnified. My reaching out for sangha is fueled by this turn of events as I am forming new relationships and re-establishing old ones. I ask myself hard questions. Do I truly want all beings to be happy? Yes. Do I see how my self-centeredness is causing me distress? Yes. Can I allow room for my feelings. I hope so. Lovers can come and go. Love can change and grow. The field of Oneness is unaffected.

My challenge is to not make a big deal out of this transition and to offer my assistance however I can to those in my ever expanding circle, and to do so joyfully, remembering that light, life and love are limitless. I can use this painful knot in my hara as a meditation object to focus my awareness and to thoroughly appreciate the treacherousness and uncertainty of samsara. Now that my heart has suffered a breaking I can more fully appreciate and hope in the song lyrics of the Zenist Leonard Cohen: "There is a crack in everything. That's how the light gets in." I am taking solace in Dharma writings, which are effective medicine, and in Sangha fellowship, which is a true life-support. I came upon a great link: *http://en.m.wikipedia.org/wiki/Paritta.* It explains the Buddhist practice of chanting verses and listening to verses for protection and blessing. To quote from Wikipedia:

> "The Buddha and the arahants (the Consummate Ones) can concentrate on the paritta suttas without the aid of another. However, when they are ill, it is easier for them to listen to what

others recite, and thus focus their minds on the dhamma that the suttas contain, rather than think of the dhamma by themselves. There are occasions, as in the case of illness, which weaken the mind (in the case of worldlings), when hetero-suggestion has been found to be more effective than autosuggestion. In the Gilana Sutta, even the Buddha Himself had the Seven Factors of Enlightenment recited to him by another monk to recover from a grave illness."

Wow! To know that even the Buddha relied upon the Sangha to recover his health is awe-inspiring and most encouraging. It reminds me of the tales in Gaudiya Vaishnavism about Radha recovering her senses when she was paralyzed (either from the overwhelming joy of seeing her Beloved Krishna or from the desperate pain of being separated from her Beloved Krishna) by her friend(s) speaking the name of Krishna into her ear. Radha is considered the Supreme Goddess, and is not separate from Krishna, the Supreme God. So even the Great Goddess, that tradition teaches, needs her friends to speak the Truth to her in order for her to keep going. It is perhaps no coincidence that our ear is not only responsible for our sense of hearing, but also our sense of balance. Hearing the Dharma from the Sangha conveys the Truth to us and keeps us in balance. *Gassho!*

PERSISTENCE IN ONE'S PRACTICE
Ken Kenyo Haile

I would like to begin my Dharma thought with the following quote:

> "Nothing in this world can take the place of persistence. Talent will not; nothing is more common than unsuccessful people with talent. Genius will not; unrewarded genius is almost a proverb. Education will not; the world is full of educated derelicts. Persistence and determination alone are omnipotent. The slogan "press on" has solved and always will solve the problems of the human race" ~ Calvin Coolidge[1].

Persistence is mentioned as the most important aspect of one's accomplishments. To be knocked down 70 times and to get up again.

> "If I had to select one quality, one personal characteristic that I regard as being most highly correlated with success, whatever the field, I would pick the trait of persistence. Determination. The will to endure to the end, to get knocked down seventy times and get up off the floor saying. "Here comes number seventy-one!" ~ Richard M. Devos[2].

I remember my early times of learning to ride a bike. The exhilaration of freedom was tremendous! I could go to places independently. I felt that I could conquer the world! During this time, I learned about the variation of effort required to move from one point to another. My bike trails were filled with small valleys and hills.

I had not noticed this before because I was traveling by car. The extra "pedal" or gas required to climb a valley was unnoticeable to me. But, pedaling a bike I noticed the variation of effort I had to use in order to climb the valley. I also noticed the excitement of going down the hill. Much less effort was required and usually I went faster than when I was pedaling.

Life is also full of hills and valleys. At times, we can enjoy the results of our efforts. Things fall into place and we happily see the accomplishments of goals we have established. It is a good time – a time to celebrate – for other valleys lie before us which will require more effort to travel. The wisdom of Yin and Yang – black and white – effort and no effort comes into play. Though seemingly apart, they are all one with different manifestations of the same essence. We cannot know about the one without knowing about the other.

One translation of the sixth step of the Buddhist eight-fold path says 'that therapy must go forth at the "staying speed," that is the critical velocity that can be sustained.'

When some aspects of our practice seem to be a challenge it is good to think that we are climbing up from the valley and that, with persistence, we shall be soon sailing down the other side.

1   http://daringtolivefully.com/perseverance-quotes
2   http://daringtolivefully.com/perseverance-quotes

TO BEAR BARE BEING
Ajita Choyo

I have been contemplating the word "bare" for the last couple weeks. The word appeared as a mistype I made for bhuta and I took the opportunity to investigate this idea of bareness as it relates to Dharma practice. For some reason I have been forced to deal with bareness in my daily life in a more intensified manner. For instance, just this past week I was ordained a deacon/servant in the Coptic Orthodox Church. I also looked at x-rays and CAT scans of my chest in my doctor's office. My girlfriend broke up with me. I either lost or had my wallet stolen. Plus, I am still mourning the loss of a pet who passed away a few weeks ago.

I want to look at a few meanings of the sound BARE. To bare is to open up to view. To be bare is to be naked. To bear is to give birth to or to keep and carry. A bear is an animal which as a totem represents awakening the great power of the unconscious. I would like to correlate these different meanings with the four alchemical imperatives: to dare, to will, to know, to keep silent.

To dare to be bare (as in naked and vulnerable; to go with empty hands).
To will to bear (to give birth to) the consciousness of Oneness
(Buddha/Christ consciousness).
To know Bear medicine (as in animal totem spirituality).
To bear (as in keep and carry) silence.

Let me also relate this to the contemplative stages of surrender, purgation, illumination and union, or sharanam, sila, prajna, samadhi.

When we Buddhists dare to be bare we surrender, to take sharanam, and entrust ourself to the Triple Gem. Or Pure Landers entrust ourselves to the simplicity of the Nembutsu.

To truly will to birth Buddha Mind one must go through the stage of purgation, of self-emptying, or uprooting the unwholesome roots, by practicing sila or moral discipline.

To know the power of Bear medicine is to experience illumination, or prajna, the awakening of the power of the Self.

To keep and carry silence is to abide in samadhi, the unitive state. This week I am privileged to have received a scholarship to attend a rhythm music course at St. Francis University and the rule when one makes a mistake is "smile and keep going." I recall the Bright Dawn "keep going" teaching and Thich Nhat Hanh's teaching to "smile and go slowly." To smile at mistakes and seeming imperfections is to loosen back into the natural state of bareness, sole Oneness. What I wish to emphasize is just that one cannot flow if one is not bare (empty handed). And the bareness bears fullness. (You can note B/F and R/L sound shift pun in BeaR or BaRe and FuLL. One cannot keep going if one is clinging or resisting the bare nature (shunyata) of Reality as it is. One will find it hard to bear the burden of consciousness, one will suffer, if one is not entrusting oneself to this most sacred and mysterious bareness.

I know this is not any new insight but it is a teaching I am being forced to accept on a deeper level. Let me leave you with some thoughts on the syllables in the word BARE. BHA is Light in Sanskrit. RE is the solar deity in Egyptian. So I find light when open to the bareness. BA is also the personality in Egyptian thought and RE is the high deity so BARE is the union of ego and Self. While BARE is to open up, or loosen, REBA is to bind up (in Hebrew). So I find the alchemical key of loosing and binding within this numinous bareness.

AMITA BHA-RAY
AMRITA BAM RAM

TRUSTING THE DARKNESS
Kyle Kaiyo Williamson

My Dharma Glimpse centers around a story from the book, *Bright Dawn* by Rev. Koyo Kubose. The story goes:

> *A man was walking home at night and lost the key to his front door. He stood on his front porch and began to look around for his lost key. A friend happened by and helped him look all over the porch without success. The friend asked, "Can you remember approximately where you lost the key?" The man said, "It was probably on the walk leading up to my front porch." The friend exclaimed, "Then why were you looking on the porch?!" The man replied, "Well, the light is better here." (Kubose, 27-28)*

This was the first time I was exposed to this story and it resonated with me, it felt as if it was speaking directly to me, as all good tales do. So I did a little research on this story—Wikipedia saves the day—and found it to be prevalent across cultures. The 13th-Century Sufi sage, Nasreddin, related a similar tale in his sermons. In a modern psychological context, David Freeman coined the term 'streetlight effect,' based on another version of the story. Streetlight effect is defined as a type of observational bias where people only look for whatever they are searching by looking where it is easiest.

There is a commercial for a hotel chain and their motto is "we'll leave the light on for you." In this context, the light is safe and welcome, but it is transient. One doesn't remain in that space forever; they return to the 'darkness' after their stay.

For me, the process of looking up information about this story is an example of my streetlight effect. I found something in this story that deeply interested me, so the first thing I do is investigate it intellectually. Looking at things through the lens of academia is comforting, because it's what I know. I work in academia and I am a student in academia.

In examining this process, I realize that I am looking at the history of the story, parallels in other cultures, and modern interpretations, but I am not looking at the actual story itself. I am clearly avoiding the message this story conveys, because it is uncomfortable. The story asks me to go out of my comfort zone the light (the intellectual academic view) and into the uncomfortable darkness (the experiential and affective realm).

So, will you join me as I step away from the light and look for the key?

JUST ONE LETTER; JUST ONE WORD
Ajita Choyo

As we consider inter-religious dialogue this week, I thought it would be insightful to consider the impact that one single letter can have on the world and our own spiritual understanding and practice. When Shakyamuni placed the letter "a", a negative prefix, to the word "atta", the Buddhist worldview could be said to have be born. (Since "atta" starts with an "a" grammar dictates that "an" be used as the formal prefix.) Now, what this this term "anatta" means exactly is still being debated, and different teachers and traditions take different positions. And again it is often just one letter that is at the center of the debate. Take for instance the presence or absence of the letter "t". Does "anatta" mean "no self" or "not self"?

What a big difference there is between the ontological position that there is no True Self (no self) and the psycho-spiritual therapeutic position that nothing should be clung to as self so as to avoid suffering (not-self). Yet both camps call themselves Buddhist. And I am sure there are many more variations and explanations of what "anatta" means. For instance, Thich Nhat Hanh translates it as "inter-being", which I think is very nice to capturing the spirit, though not so literal a translation. A local lay Buddhist in my area who represents Buddhism in inter-faith settings refers to "anatta" as "soullessness", and I have expressed concern to him about this because of the English connotations of being soulless. It can imply being heartless and so I suggested without success that he use the word "selflessness" which has positive connotations in English. Also, most Americans are familiar with the science of psychology, so to represent Buddhism in inter-faith settings as affirming there is no soul or psyche could make persons think that Buddhism is anti-scientific. I am of the view that the "no-selfers" veer toward nihilism and metaphysical speculation, but accept anyone who takes refuge in the Triple Gem to be Buddhist, and believe that we need to be respectful of the diversity within religious traditions while at the same time advocating our personal position on the authentic teachings of our religious founder.

Let us look now at the most troubling letter which is at the center of spiritual studies: "I". Note in your personal life how one naturally reacts when one's "I"-ness is threatened, often from just one word being spoken about you or a loved one. Buddhists, if not all spiritual seekers, should know that suffering results from clinging to anything as "I, me, mine". Hindus teach the practice of "neti, neti", meaning recognizing that I am "not this, not that". Buddhist teach "anatta". Muslims teach "fanaa" or extinction. Christians teach self-emptying / kenosis. (For you linguists out there, note how the beginning of shunya corresponds to the beginning of kenosis; soft "sh" to hard "k" aspirate soundshift, same "n" sound, same root meaning of "empty".)

Since we are Westerners, let's look at our own western history. In the Christian world the first great Christian schism occurred over just one letter. At the Council of Chalcedon the bishops of the West and East opposed the bishops of the Orient. Chalcedon affirmed that Christ is in (en) two natures (human and divine), while the Oriental position that lost out held that Christ is from out of (ek) two natures (into one nature, the nature of the incarnate Logos). Considering the non-dual emphasis of oriental traditions, it is not surprising that the bishops of the Oriental churches held to their guns about Christ having one nature, and this position makes more sense to me. The later schism between the Western Catholic and Eastern Orthodox churches was largely the result of not one letter, but one phrase, "and the Son", which was added to the Nicene Creed by the Roman bishop without consulting the other bishops.

Unfortunately there was violence that erupted and suffering that ensued from these theological disputes over language, as is too often the case. It is my hope in sharing these thoughts that we can understand how just one letter can change a religious teaching completely. May we thus make more mindful effort to understand the original spirit of our respective religious founders so as to be able to translate this spirit into our contemporary regional vocabulary, while at the same recognizing and appreciating our unity in diversity.

Gassho.

THE STARTING LINE IS THE FINISHING LINE
Kyle Kaiyo Williamson

I am not a very physically active person but this year I decided to change that and work toward being more body aware through physical fitness. To keep this motivation I decided that I want to participate in a 5k later on in the year. I am not doing it for competition, I don't want to place, I simply want to participate and finish. To accomplish this goal I asked the resources around me for help.

My partner, (the resource) is physically active and goes to the Gym, Aikido Dojo and does 5k's. After talking with him we came up with a plan that works for me. My work schedule does not coincide with the gym schedule and membership is not cheap, so that is not an option. There is a phone app (Couch to 5k) that monitors progress and creates goals to work toward to help advance your progress.

I am still in the earlier stages of the program and I jog/walk 3 times a week slowly increasing the amount of time I jog while decreasing the amount of time I walk. Soon I will be adding strength training to this cardio program for overall fitness.

I must be careful at this stage as I have not committed to a specific race and my deadline remains loose and unfixed. If I feel I am not progressing enough I may push back the race date. I may push this date back indefinitely because I simply do not have confidence in my performance ability, making it easier to be stuck in the conditioning stage and could never progress beyond it. Running by myself is easier because there is no chance at failure.

This is letting fear take hold and run my life. I need to remind myself that if I keep up my exercise goal I should be ready to participate in a 5k by October. If I should 'fail' by not finishing the race that is ok; at least I undertook the race. I can (and should) undertake another race at this point because the physical conditioning has become a habit, and having another race will keep my motivation.

The stages of the race become less and less distinct in their level of importance; the finish line becomes just as important as the starting line. Exercising is just something you do, not a chore and not an endorphin rush, but a part of living.

This process of preparing for the race is very similar to the process one undertakes toward Nirvana. The first part of the process is the realization that life as presented is lacking and unfulfilling. We really can't buy our way into happiness. Once we know we want to understand what is truly fulfilling, we seek out an expert on the subject. The expert can be the Buddhist Sutta/Sutra, commentaries, and of course a physical Sensei or Guru.

With the basic information obtained from the expert, one can begin a practice or the conditioning part of preparing for a 5K. The various practices one undertakes toward the achievement of Nirvana, such as precepts, chants, meditation, entrusting and visualizations, are similar to the cardio and strength training workouts that a new participant may undertake.

Again it is at the practice stage that we may grow stagnant in our development. If we focus on our failures during our practices we may find that we are essentially pushing Nirvana further and further away. If we accept our failings as part of the experience, we may get past them, transcend them even. Hopefully our practice will help us uncover the wisdom and compassion of the Buddha-Mind helping us to realize Nirvana. When we have that moment of clarity we will begin to see things non-dualistically; the journey is the goal, the practice (the means) is enlightenment (the ends), Nirvana is Samsara, the starting line is the finish line.

A MI TA :
Ajita Choyo

Gassho Sangha! Infinite Light of Amita Nam!

I would like, if I may, marvel and play with the Infinite Name Amita (or Amida in Japanese, as opposed to Sanskrit). One may refer to Truth as the Holy Name, Hari Nam, the True Name, Sat Nam, the Infinite Name, Amita Nam, Nembutsu, etc... Many Mahayana traditions focus upon the Amita name, which has the three syllables A MI TA.

"A" translates as "Not." "Mita" translates as "meted out, measured, defined, limited." So Amita is thus the immeasurable, the infinite, the undefinable, the unlimited. It is my understanding that the Name of Amita is not different from Amita-bha Buddha. This Limitless Luminous Mystery within the Infinite Name Amida is something akin to trans-rational experience. Limitlessness beyond qualifications is a core aspect of mystery. (Karl Rahner, the 20th century Jesuit theologian, recommended that the term "God" be replaced with "Ultimate Mystery" for many decades.) The MI syllable in AMIDA for me brings to mind the MYO syllable (in the Daimoku) which means Mysterious. It also brings to my mind the Word, the Great Self, the True ME, the Mahatman.

I am told that the prefix A can, in addition to meaning "not," also mean "great," two polar opposite meanings. So Amida could read as the Great Measure, or Measure of Measures. The A syllable is commonly associated with oneness. It is also considered the origin, the source. In fact, if one reads AMITA backwards one discovers ADI MA, the Original Mother. In Buddhism original non-production, 'ady-anutpada' is associated with A. In Dzogchen, Ah is the source of all mantras, of all light and sound. The TA syllable can refer to Tathata, or Thusness. (In the DA form it may refer to Dana or giving.) I also liken it to ShunyaTA as it is the ending syllable on the word. AMITA could therefore be read as Not-Me-Thus or Great-Me-Thus.

From reading about the esoteric meaning of Amita I learned that A is considered the cause, MI is linked to the practice, and TI is seen as the Buddha. Thus I find in AMITA the Ground (A), the Path (MI), and the Fruit (TA). Genshin of Mt. Hei (942-1017) proposed a theory that A, MI, and TA represents the triple truth of the void, the temporary, and the middle; Kakuban likewise wrote: 'The practicer of the Single Path of the Unconditioned (i.e., one who follows the Tendai teaching) contemplates the void, the temporary, and the middle through the contemplation of A, MI, and TA.' One can thus discover Nirvana, Samsara and Oneness in the name Amita.

Since we are in an American context let us refer here to Joseph Rael's teachings on Tiwa Native American spirituality in reference to the sacred meaning of sounds (from his book *Tracks of Dancing Light*):

A - washing, purity, purification, purifying light
M - to bring forth, manifesting, matter
I – awareness
(**D** - doing, creating, creation, throwing light)
T - time, crystallized light, speeding light that is slowed down light
A - washing, purity, purification, purifying light

So according to Rael's sound mysticism Amita may mean The Purifying Light manifesting awareness, time washing. Amida could mean The Purifying Light manifesting awareness, creating purity.

This is a chart of some of the Buddhist associations for these three syllables. The chart is from the book *A Buddhist Theory of Semiotics* by Fabio Rambelli.

Let me conclude with the chorus from a recent song by the Zen songwriter Leonard Cohen, from the song "Born in Chains":

Word of Words
And Measure of all Measures
Blessed is the Name
The Name be blessed
Written on my heart
In burning Letters
That's all I know
I cannot read the rest

Bright Dawn Dharma Glimpses:

BRIGHT DAWN TRAILBLAZER'S
In Memoriam

*With a heavy heart, we let you know that **Linda Shoyo Sensei** passed away in November, 2016, at Plymouth, Wisconsin. She, along with her husband David, were members of our LM5 class. They completed the Lay Ministry Program and came to the Bright Dawn Center in Coarsegold, California for the LM5 Induction Ceremony in May, 2013. Linda's Dharma Name, SHOYO, means "Smiling Sun." We like to think that she shared the same warm serenity reflected in the gentle smile depicted on Gautama Buddha statues.*

*Sadly, **Marge Shakayo Sensei** passed away about 6 months after being inducted as a Bright Dawn Center Lay Minister in May 2015. Her memory lives on as the one who uplifted her LM7 class with her cheerful "Aloha" at each Sunday conference call throughout the Lay Ministry program. More importantly, Marge Shakayo Sensei set an example for us all as she struggled with cancer off and on during the two year Lay Ministry program by maintaining and sharing her positive attitude with us all.*

Bright Dawn Dharma Glimpses:

A GRATITUDE BOW & GASSHO

It is with deep pleasure and gratitude that I served as Bright Dawn Trailblazer President for the year 2016.

Forever will I be grateful for the Bright Dawn Lay Minister's training program. My thanks to both Rev. Koyo & Adrienne Kubose for tirelessly giving of themselves to carrying on the legacy of the late Rev. Gyomay Kubose by promoting the core teaching of The Way of Oneness especially through the Lay Minister training program. This open and eclectic approach has helped me to mature into my spiritual journey in ways I did not know possible. Learning to approach relationships and situations in my life through the lens of Dharma has helped me tremendously.

Thank you Rev. Koyo sensei and Adrienne sensei for all you have given of your time and self, freely and without condition other than for students to commit to their own personal growth.

Thank you to William Toyo sensei for the suggestion of creating this Dharma Glimpse book, a platform so that Bright Dawn Lay Minister's voices of everyday suchness can be shared.

A special thank you to Eli Blyden of CrunchTimeGraphics.com for your friendship and professional services.

Thank you to all of the Bright Dawn Lay Ministers who submitted their Dharma Glimpses and also who participated in editing the many essays. This book project was indeed a community effort.

I am very encouraged and inspired to be a part of such a multifaceted and wholly inclusive group of people who are committed to not only their own Dharma awakening but committed to shining their light to help others to awaken as well.

No matter what lies before us, greater is that which lies at our center within.

In the words of Rev. Koyo sensei, *"KEEP GOING!"*

Tamu Hoyo Ngina
Bright Dawn Trailblazer President 2016
Autumn, 2016

Made in the USA
Monee, IL
11 May 2020